WOMEN ON TOP

Women, Wealth & Social Change

By Haleh Moddasser, CPA

ISBN: 978-0-578-64545-2
Printed in the United States of America

Dedication

To our children, and their children, all of whom
deserve a kinder, gentler and more sustainable world.

Acknowledgements

This book would not have been possible without the support of my diligent and deeply engaged editor, Emily Crookston; my publisher, Michelle Kulp, and my band of women clients who provide me with context, reality checks and immense joy.

Table of Contents

Foreword

Haleh Moddasser, like me, has learned to function in a very narrow subset of personal finance usually reserved for men. We are both financial advisors who specialize in helping boomer women navigate a world they rarely inhabit: money management. Yes, we women know how to spend it, but more importantly, we now know how to earn it. While our mothers usually earned an income that supplemented our fathers', that status quo has been steadily eroded by women who are earning, saving, and investing money for our own financial independence. We are now the first generation of women with seven-figure investment portfolios of our own. In addition, we are inheriting money either through the death of our spouses or our parents. Now, we *must* learn how to invest it in a way that helps us *and* our world.

As Haleh points out in this joyous book of seizing the power of the money we have, we can finally use our wealth to make a BIG difference in this world. Through Environmental, Social, and Governance (ESG) investing (she'll explain…), we can go beyond the usual roles of volunteerism, political activism and charitable donations to a more powerful role of investing in companies whose corporate cultures are reflective of the values we share.

It's heart stopping, breathtaking, and deeply rewarding to know there is a way for us as women to support and encourage change in this world for the good. And our legacies will bear that out if we learn how to work together to invest our money in companies we love.

After writing her first book, _Gray Divorce, Silver Linings: A Woman's Guide to Divorce After 50_, Haleh was a guest on my podcast, *Power of the Purse,* where she shared with me the premise of the book you are now reading. I couldn't wait to get my hands on it and take a deep dive into how ESG investing really works. It's a delicious way to get in the back door and see how your money can make the needle move.

Congratulations, Haleh! I'm very proud to say I know you and support what you are doing.

Lynn S. Evans, CFP®

Preface

The 2019 Women, Wealth, and ESG Study

In preparation for writing this book, I conducted an original research study utilizing a third-party research firm.

In the study, approximately 500 women from across the United States, ages 55-75 with investable assets of $500,000 or more were surveyed to garner their opinions about social issues, women's wealth and women's ability to influence social change.

The results of the study are incorporated throughout this book, and a full copy of the study along with its methodology can be found in Appendix A.

Introduction

I wasn't the kind of kid who would start UNICEF. Nor did I ever dream of changing the world. In fact, as an immigrant coming of age in the United States, my daily struggle was one of simply trying to fit in.

Things might have been different if my family were from one of the countries we in the West admire—like England or France, or maybe Switzerland, where I imagined people skied and lived in mountain-top chalets. But I am from Iran. And I was in high school during the Iranian hostage crisis when 52 American diplomats and citizens were held hostage for 444 days.

On each of those days, my parents, sister, and I would anxiously gather around the TV to watch the crisis unfold on network television. While most people in the United States watched the same footage with keen interest, the clashing of cultures and governments was more personal for me. I watched with horror the images of Iranians portrayed on the news, knowing that these images would forever supplant the images of the Iran I knew. For example, the image of my great-grandfather, the tea merchant who traveled the Silk Road while building a family empire. Or my great grandmother who founded a school for girls 110 years ago that is still in existence today. Overnight, it seemed, my integrated world began to fracture and my heritage, as embodied by my parents and the stories they would tell, began to conflict sharply with the brave new world holding the promise of the American woman I would become.

I struggled hard to make sense of what I saw on the news, the rendition of the "facts" differing greatly from those shared by my relatives back "home." Often it seemed the footage was staged for political effect, as a way to demonize an entire nation. All the while,

I knew the news stories didn't accurately depict the people or culture of Iran. But without widespread access to non-Western news sources, the domestic storyline prevailed. At least today with the internet, we have easy access to the foreign press and potentially a different perspective on global events. But in the 1980s, it was easier for the powers that be to spread their singular version of events.

As expected, the media frenzy generated nothing but deep divides and great animosity between the citizens of each country, not to mention their governments. For me, these artificial and politically motivated divides between people did not exist. What I experienced were people, regardless of race, gender, or national origin, all simply trying to live their best lives given their unique circumstances. But the conflict persisted, and each nightly news broadcast began with an updated count which spawned the career of a young Ted Koppel[1]: "Day 365 with the hostages..." followed by "Day 366 with the hostages..." and so on. From my point of view, both sides were completely misunderstood. My sense of justice was deeply offended by the racism and hatred I witnessed during this period, and my sense of cynicism over politics and the media ignited.

I realized then that the media was not purely a mechanism for transmitting information; it was also a medium that could color the thoughts of an entire nation. Looking back, it was this experience that motivated my decision to become a journalism major in college—thinking somehow I could right this wrong. After all, wasn't it the role of the media to educate the public about what was happening in the world free from political bias? Little did I know that some 40 years later, the media would have become even more polarizing, this time dividing Americans amongst themselves.

As the years went by, I gradually left my heritage behind. I went away to college, married an American, and had two beautiful children, all the while distancing myself from the painful experiences of my adolescence. The lessons of my youth, however, never fully left me. As a young mother, I often thought about the kind of world my children would inherit. I wanted to make it kinder, gentler and more just. As crazy as it may sound, I thought about these things while waiting in the carpool line at school, while cooking dinner — the news blaring in the background, our Bernese Mountain Dog barking. I continually sought a way, any way, to make a difference. Maybe I could write, I thought, or teach. I wondered if it was even possible for me to effectively communicate what I had experienced.

Despite my good intentions, however, it was nearly impossible to do much of anything other than care for my children in those early years. I was busy volunteering my time at school functions and bringing hot lunches to class. And, of course, I was especially concerned with teaching my children how to treat all people with respect and empathy. But truth be told, my circle of influence was really quite small. Being a mom was, after all, a full-time job. When the school bell rang at three o'clock, my children—eyes bright, cheeks flushed—would bounce into the minivan that had become our world. Excitedly, the three of us would embark on the after-school adventure of the day: the make-believe story of days long gone, the garden we would plant, the games we would play. And for better or worse, my thoughts about changing the broader world would once again take a backseat to the skinned knee, the much-needed hug, and the alluring bedtime story that always ended with a "happily ever after." On each and every one of those days, my singular focus was the two little people under my charge.

It was not until many years later, when my children were adults, that I began to revisit my earlier dreams about making our world better. I considered journalism as a career but was far too disillusioned by the state of the media. Instead, through a confluence of many circumstances, I found a career that I believed could make a real difference — one woman at a time. I became a financial advisor specializing in helping other women in my newfound situation...

divorced and single. My goal was to empower these women financially. It was important work and very satisfying. But at the end of the day, I still couldn't shake the desire to do something bigger.

Ironically, this journey has made me realize that I'm not alone in my quest to make the world just a little bit better. As a partner of a wealth management firm, with a practice devoted primarily to women, I have come to realize that my clients *all* long for a greater sense of purpose and meaning. Having retired from successful careers, raised children, effectively lived full and complete lives, these women are deeply concerned about the world the next generation will inherit. We have all, in our own way, come to realize that no amount of money, time, or recreation will satisfy the desire to accomplish something greater than ourselves and to leave a lasting legacy for those we love. I no longer wonder whether my singular voice can make a difference; I now realize it is the collective call of women just like me, and you, that can and will change the world.

Values-Based Investing:
How to Harness Women's Collective Power

The ongoing question, however, is "How?" How can we women best harness our collective desire to make a positive impact in a world plagued by social injustice? In truth, many of us are finding the old ways stale, if not ineffective. Neither the ballot box nor our charitable endeavors have yielded the results for which we had hoped. In fact, my research indicates that regardless of party affiliation, most American boomer women today who, as we'll see, control the majority of the nation's wealth, don't believe that either politics or philanthropy, alone, can fix the social problems we face. In the Women, Wealth, and ESG survey, conducted in preparation for the writing of this book, I confirmed that only 28% of respondents believe the U.S. political system can solve our social problems. When asked if nonprofits or charities can solve our social issues, the results were only marginally better, with only 33% of respondents believing such organizations alone can right size the social issues we face. Everything from slowing climate change to reducing gender inequality to reducing gun violence seems tied to the all mighty dollar, as opposed to a greater sense of social responsibility.

Fortunately, it appears—thanks to the nascent power of social media and collective outrage over little to no progress being made on social issues we care about—that ordinary Americans are finding ways to make their voices heard outside of these traditional channels.

This first occurred to me in the weeks following the Parkland, Florida school shooting on February 14, 2018. In that incident, a former high school student opened fire with a semi-automatic rifle at Marjory Stoneman Douglas High School killing 17 people and injuring 14 others. Almost immediately, calls began to come into my office from clients, both men and women, asking that our portfolio managers sell all positions related to the gun industry. A search of our investment vehicles revealed that we held stock in several national retailers selling semi-automatic rifles and bump stocks, including Walmart and Dick's Sporting Goods. As requested, we divested these holdings.

Of course, our clients weren't the only ones using their dollars and voices to express outrage. Infuriated Americans everywhere followed the lead of the high school students at Marjory Stoneman Douglas, who had lost friends that day, and took to social media. Bad publicity gone viral suddenly resulted in both reputational and economic risk for corporations. As a result, Dick's Sporting Goods ended sales of all assault-style rifles, and Walmart raised the minimum age to purchase guns and ammunition from 18 to 21—all within a two-week period. For the first time, we saw real change following a mass shooting—no politicians, no lobbying, no NRA, no debate.

Done.

The reaction on social media was tremendous and unprecedented. Here are some examples from a Twitter feed:

> *"Apparently, the young people of Parkland have made an impact. YES! Dick's has developed a social conscience when will the politicians follow suit?"* <u>Kathy Larit</u>

> *"Businesses have to take into their own hands what the government can't do."* <u>Allison Joy</u>

> *"A step in the right <u>direction</u>... I will order something from Dick's online today."* <u>Ellen, California</u>

To be fair, gun rights advocates also tweeted their disapproval. However, the positive hits were far more prevalent. While it's hard to know whether Dick's Sporting Goods was moved more by conscience or greed, one thing was imminently clear: the court of public opinion, coupled with economic threat, had made an impact—and a far more effective one than all the political wrangling surrounding this issue over the years. The price of Dick's stock went up 2% following the announcement of the change in gun policy.

How powerful. I experienced at that moment what I had instinctively known all along:

Public sentiment, if channeled economically,
can impact corporate behavior.

That day, I witnessed a power unleashed that promised a more direct route to change. And for the first time, I realized the potential of values-based investing—a type of investing with a dual mandate:

To do good while also doing well.

Not wanting to wait for another senseless tragedy, I immediately began seeking a more proactive, deliberate way to harness this power. I found there are several options available for those who want to channel their economic power and their values toward changing social policy. One approach in particular has blossomed in recent years with the promise of gaining unprecedented traction. It's commonly referred to as ESG investing, short for Environmental, Social, and Governance investing. ESG is a type of investing that broadly incorporates the following criteria when evaluating public companies in which to invest:

- Environmental factors: these include corporate behaviors that impact the climate, waste and energy

- Social factors: these criteria involve the way a corporation treats its customers, vendors, and employees and includes issues such as human rights, labor, and safety policies

- Governance factors: these focus on the way a company is governed including its corporate transparency, diversity, and executive compensation policies

We'll take a deeper dive into each of these areas later in the book. For now, it's important to note that these criteria, when combined with standard investment analysis, are increasingly thought to produce equal, if not better, long term performance while also promoting better practices by corporate entities.[2] This type of dual mandate investing, while not new, is rapidly gaining traction. What was once labeled anti-Capitalist by economists like Milton Friedman, who believed the only role for companies was to generate profits and was later viewed only as a "niche" investment philosophy, has now become mainstream.

ESG Investing - the Real Women's Empowerment Movement

Today, it is easier than ever to use your financial resources to have a real social impact while continuing to grow your nest egg. In the 1990s, those who wanted to steer their investments in socially conscious ways likely had to accept lower financial returns in exchange for trying to make a difference. Now, nearly 30 years later, there's good evidence to suggest that investors can achieve comparable returns. In fact, it appears that companies prioritizing Environmental, Social, and Governance (ESG) policies perform as well or better than those who do not.[3] And, of course, when companies do better, their shareholders do better.

"This is it," I thought to myself.

This is the answer to how women can work together to make the world better — to make a real difference — while financially empowering themselves. ESG is the *real* women's empowerment movement!

Imagine, I thought, if women, who are currently responsible for 85% of all purchases and influence 70-80% of all consumer spending,[4] wielded their economic power *en masse*. This idea so excited me that I could hardly sleep. As a woman working in a male-dominated field, I know all too well the challenges of trying to make it in a man's world. Only about one in five financial advisors is a woman.[5] In 2019, just 6.6% of companies in the Fortune 500 had a female CEO.[6] Women now represent just over 20% of the board seats at the top 3,000 publicly traded companies in the U.S.[7] A woman has never been President of the United States. And yet, in the area of wealth, I realized that women are already the ones on top. This means we actually have the economic power to make a difference — *now*. All we have to do is exercise it.

Now, if it's surprising to you that women have this kind of latent power, let me shed some more light here. This fact doesn't typically make the nightly news, but the reality is, in America, women currently control between 51%-60% of the nation's wealth, depending on the study referenced.[8] And experts estimate this number will rise to 67% by the year 2030.[9]

How is this possible, you ask?

To start with, baby boomers are the wealthiest generation in history. And because of what is commonly referred to as the "double-inheritance," boomer women, in particular, stand to inherit wealth both from their parents and their husbands within the next decade.

In addition, boomers are divorcing in unprecedented numbers. The so-called "gray divorce"— a divorce between long-time married couples over the age of 50—results in an even greater transfer of wealth from men to women of this generation at an even younger age than widowhood. Add to all this women's rising earnings power (affecting all generations of women), and it's easy to see why women suddenly hold unprecedented wealth and power, albeit untapped.

Let's put these statistics into context: by 2020, women are expected to control approximately $22 trillion.[10] Note that the entire national GDP of Australia in 2018 was only $1.4 trillion USD.[11] The Congressional Budget Office (CBO) projects that the U.S. annual deficit will hit $1 trillion in 2020.[12] And in 2019, our total national debt is more than $23 trillion and rising.[13]

Indeed, the wealth and power women wield is massive.

If all of this is news to you, you're not alone. Few Americans— least of all women themselves—realize women wield such economic power. Based on my *Women, Wealth, and ESG* survey, women believe they control only 36% of the nation's wealth!

Note: it's important not to confuse "wealth" with income here. That women control more of the wealth than men does not mean we, as a society, have solved the gender pay gap. Women continue to earn, on average, 79 cents on the dollar relative to their white male counterparts, and that's if you're a white woman. It's just 67 cents for black women and 58 cents for Latina women.[14] I'll discuss the distinction between wealth and income in more detail in Chapter 1, but "wealth," in this context, is defined as investable assets in excess of $500,000 that has accrued to women through inheritance, divorce settlements, and their own earnings.

Women and Wealth Statistics

- Women are responsible for 85% of purchases in the U.S.
- Women control 70-80% of all consumer spending in the U.S.
- Women currently control 51-60% of the nation's wealth, and experts predict the number will rise to 67% by 2030[15]
- Women believe they control 36% of the nation's wealth
- $14-$22 trillion in wealth is expected to transfer to boomer women in the next decade

Now is the Time to Put Our Unprecedented Wealth to Work

Given these statistics, the case for leveraging our wealth *now* is even more compelling. History has shown that opportunities to create lasting, systemic change are infrequent and often fleeting. In this case, there are reasons to believe that women won't have the ability to singularly impact social change for long, since as boomer women die, their wealth will pass to their children, both male and female. In addition, it's likely that cultural, social, and generational differences between boomers, Gen X-ers, and millennials will result in a more even distribution of wealth moving forward.

Which brings us to the topic of this book: for at least the next few decades, we boomer women are positioned to use our unprecedented wealth in a unique and powerful way. Using ESG criteria to direct our investment dollars, we can reshape the issues we care about most deeply, bypassing political gridlock and going directly to those we believe can make the difference—the business community. And, more importantly, I believe the desire for change is there. I see it in my clients and my research provides the data to support my experience.

Again, according to my Women, Wealth, and ESG survey, only 28% of women, ages 55 to 75, with assets over $500,000, agree or strongly agree with the statement, "The U.S. political system has the ability to solve our social problems" and only slightly more (33%) agree or strongly agree that nonprofits and charities have the ability to solve our social problems. By contrast, 61% agree or strongly agree that public and private companies have this ability. That is, roughly double the number of women in my survey believe companies are in a better position to impact our social issues than either government or philanthropy alone. And, fortunately, women have the unprecedented wealth and power to propel that change — *now.* We no longer have to wait for political gridlock to end and hope that more women gain leadership positions (though gaining this type of power is also on our agendas) or sit back and hope that nonprofits doing amazing work will get the funding they need to bring about the kind of social change we want. We now have a third way to propel social change.

Are you fed up with watching politicians and leaders in D.C. fail to bring about change? Do you feel like your money could be doing more good in the world? Are you looking for a way to make a bigger impact than donating to charity, volunteering your time, or writing to your local representatives? This book will show you how to do more with your wealth.

I'm on a mission to help you and women just like you change the world.

Join me.

CHAPTER 1

Women Have the Power, We Just Don't Realize It

I've worked with hundreds of women in my role as a financial advisor. Some are living paycheck to paycheck, while others have hundreds of millions of dollars in assets (I'm not exaggerating). In spite of this, I've met exactly zero women who *feel* "rich." In fact, they all seem to have one thing in common…a desperate fear of becoming a bag lady.

My theories over the years about why women fear the loss of financial security above all else have ranged from a primitive need to have a man "take care" of us to how society has trained women to believe they'll never have or be enough. It's hard to deny that from the moment a woman emerges from the womb, she is subliminally taught that "business, money, and finance" are the purview of men. Even if you were born into a family that encouraged money conversations, as soon as you ventured out into the world on your own, you likely encountered pushback.

As a woman, it's not very sexy to talk about money; in some circles, it's considered downright rude. Let it be known that you care about wealth and you might be dubbed an alpha female…aggressive, overpowering, greedy, and ultimately…undesirable. Clearly, these aren't the first qualities you'd think of adding to your online dating profile. No, these are qualities reserved for the most coveted of males.

And yet, women are rightfully concerned about their financial futures. On average, women can expect to live five years longer than men (81 years vs. 76 years); generally, they have earned less during their lifetimes and therefore receive lower social security checks.[16] And according to the U.S. Census Bureau, 80% of wives outlive their husbands and will lose their husband's social security income as well.[17] In fact, only 17% of women over the age of 85 are married (compared to 60% of men of the same age). Therefore, women will typically bear the costs of long-term care on their own while most men have their wives to help care for them. Hence, the near-universal fear of becoming the dreaded "bag lady" — pushing along a cart of our things, with no roof over our heads, and no one to take care of us.

Initially, I thought that perhaps as a woman over 50, working with clients over the age of 50, my views were a bit dated. Perhaps the younger generation had a more enlightened perspective. But several years ago, I had a young woman in her mid-20's working for me who was using an online dating site. She was smart, attractive, and driven, but increasingly had trouble finding a romantic partner. After two years, she finally divulged that she planned to change her profile because being a woman in the financial services industry was too unappealing for most of the men she was meeting. Either they were intimidated by her or feared they would be unable to keep up.

I know...*I know.*

Obviously, the guys she was meeting were insecure and not worth her time, but after years of searching for love, she felt she had no choice. The message was clear: as a young professional woman working in a "man's" industry, she was being told to give up her identity or be left behind.

Whatever the reason, I continue to find that many women don't invest the time or have an interest in focusing on their own financial futures. This characteristic has *nothing* to do with their level of intelligence or investing prowess. In fact, if you look at the data, women are *better* investors than men. According to LouAnn Lofton, author of *Warren Buffett Invests Like a Girl: And Why You Should, Too*, women are more cautious, take fewer risks, are less susceptible to peer pressure, do more research, and are ultimately more patient investors.[18] Although some in the industry claim that women are scared or "risk-averse," the research Lofton cites shows instead that men are actually overconfident, take more risks, and follow a herd-like mentality, all of which can lead to more frequent trading, and ultimately, lower investment returns. However, when contrasted with the stereotypical male investor, a woman's investment style can *appear* timid or shy when, in fact, it is more successful.

Now, if you're constantly told in subtle and not-so-subtle ways that you shouldn't bother with money, that it's not sexy to talk about money, or that your attitudes toward investing are too timid, how likely are you to feel rich? Really unlikely. This unspoken truth may be politically incorrect, but it is a vital reality that needs to be called out. Because, let's face it, if you don't feel rich, you most likely feel poor. And if you feel poor, you probably feel powerless, afraid and, therefore, unable to exert influence. This mindset is quite the challenge and has real implications.

My experience tracks Lofton's research, which is why I firmly believe that when it comes to wealth, women have nothing to be shy about. I marvel daily at the women I encounter. Multifaceted, well educated, daughters, mothers, wives, professionals—they generally care deeply about the greater good. These women build families and communities, yet, they lack confidence when it comes to building their own financial security.

For example, one client who has more money than she could ever spend on herself and her family in her lifetime is so afraid of making a mistake that she has refused to invest in the stock market over the past ten years. As a result, she has been on the sidelines during the longest bull market in history—passing up an opportunity to double her money. Just think about how much good she could have done had she invested and put the returns she earned into causes she cares about the most. Instead, she has spent down her assets for years and has lost 1.8% annually in purchasing power due to the power of inflation alone.[19] In effect, her fear of becoming a "bag lady" is creating a self-fulfilling prophecy. If she continues down this path, she is doing serious damage to her legacy.

Another client has trouble spending money, period. Again, she has more money than most, but is unable to enjoy "living" a little. "This is all I'll ever have," she says. "I can't *afford* to spend." This is a common fear among women, especially if they don't have a steady flow of cash coming in from a pension or another source after they retire and stop earning a salary.

These are just two examples of many. As I said, I've met exactly zero women who feel rich. The truth is, however, that even if most women don't *feel* rich individually, as a group, women today own more of the nation's wealth than at any other time in history.

What is Wealth?

So, what does it mean to be wealthy? This is an important question and one that needs a clear answer. Often, and especially in the U.S., having a high income is confused with being rich or wealthy. However, it's important to distinguish between income and wealth, as these words have distinct meanings.

Income

Income refers to your paycheck if you're working or to your social security and monthly pension if you're retired. It also encompasses alimony as well as other "passive" income streams, such as interest and dividends from your invested assets or your savings. Generally, income includes any periodic payment (i.e., weekly or monthly) that you use to fund your living expenses.

But the reality is, often those with the highest incomes also have expenses to match—and in far too many cases, their expenses exceed their incomes. So wealth is not really about income. With that said, if your income exceeds your expenses, you might actually feel "rich." You can splurge or you can save the extra money (I highly recommend the latter. Sorry.).

When discussing income, it's also important to note that while women have made great strides professionally, there is still a meaningful disparity between what women earn versus what men earn for doing essentially the same job. I mentioned the wage or income gap in the introduction, but if we're going to talk about women and wealth, we cannot ignore this disparity. Women continue to earn on average 79 cents on the dollar relative to men.[20] Some of this gap may be due to pure gender discrimination and sexism, but social scientists point to systemic reasons for the disparity.

Women bear children and are still responsible for the bulk of childcare and other domestic responsibilities in female-male households. As a result, they are less likely to want more demanding jobs, to accept travel assignments, or to be singularly focused on work during their childbearing years. And, (shockingly?) the U.S. ranks dead last among developed nations when it comes to paid parental leave benefits.[21]

Additionally, women are often less likely than their male counterparts to negotiate salaries or ask for raises (remember how it's considered socially unacceptable for women to bring up money?).

Causation aside, the reality remains that women generally earn less than men over their lifetimes. This means they save less and typically have lower social security benefits, too which may explain why women's confidence in financial matters is on the decline. For instance, a 2019 study conducted by Allianz Life Insurance Company of North America found the following:[22]

- Fewer women feel financially secure (62% in 2019 versus 68% in 2016)
- Fewer women say that they've asked for a raise at work (27% in 2019 versus 44% in 2016)
- Fewer women say they feel confident in their financial decision-making (83% in 2019 versus 91% in 2016)

Despite all this, women continue to make amazing strides professionally:

- The number of wealthy women in the U.S. is growing twice as fast as the number of wealthy men[23]
- Women represent more than 40% of all Americans with gross investable assets above $600,000[24]
- Women are the primary earners in about 40% of all families[25]
- Women represent 47% of the total workforce in the U.S.[26]
- Women are earning 57% of all undergraduate degrees, 59% of master's degrees, and 53% of doctorates[27]
- 40% of U.S. businesses are women-owned[28]

So, what's a girl to do? Well, the disconnect between women's perceptions about their own financial prowess and their professional accomplishments suggests conversations about women and wealth need to focus on financial empowerment. In my view, ESG can and should be an important part of this conversation. The advice I always give my clients is do what you can to increase your income, but don't waste a lot of energy "shaking your fist" at the injustice of the income gap. While there's little you can do as an individual to move the needle here, this is exactly the type of social issue collective action and shareholder activism through ESG can impact. I'll show you how values-aligned and ESG-integrated investing can give you and other like-minded investors a voice on issues of gender disparity (and other social issues, of course) in subsequent chapters.

Wealth

Wealth: If you follow my advice, you will focus on increasing your income, spending within your means, and accumulating wealth. In this context, *wealth* refers to your nest egg or "rainy day money." It is there to provide for you when your income is no longer available or enough. If you lose your job, get divorced, become widowed, or retire, you can utilize your wealth to fund your living expenses. The more wealth you have, the richer you may feel. That is, if you're a man. Remember…women seldom *feel* rich (even when they have accumulated more wealth than the average American).

So, how much money does it take to be rich? Well, being rich or feeling wealthy are relative terms. Because of social comparison, if you have the nicest home in your neighborhood, you're likely to feel wealthy even if the value of your home is below the national average. But setting aside complexities like this, in the United States, if you have a net worth of $500,000 you are "richer" than approximately 80% of people. This seems like a pretty good benchmark for our purposes, then, when it comes to putting a numeric value on wealth.

Consider the following chart displaying net worth by percentile:[29]

Percentile	Net Worth
10.0%	-$962.66
20.0%	$4,798.06
30.0%	$18,753.84
40.0%	$49,132.21
50.0%	$97,225.55
60.0%	$169,550.64
70.0%	$279,594.27
80.0%*	$499,263.50
90.0%*	$1,182,390.36
95.0%*	$2,377,985.22
99.0%*	$10,374,030.10

*Women control up to 60% of the nation's wealth. In this context, wealth is defined as having a minimum net worth of $500,000.

What is especially interesting in relation to the topic of this book is that depending on which study you accept, women control 51%-60% of that upper level.[30] This is all the more amazing given that women lag behind in income and have only recently made tremendous professional strides to catch up to and in some cases, surpass, men on measures that tend to yield wealth. The assets representing net worth displayed above have either been earned, inherited, or divided, as in the case of gray divorce, and currently translate into a staggering $14 to $22 trillion of wealth...and potential influence in the hands of women.[31] Again, in 2020, we are likely at the top of this range, and growing.

Understanding where women have been economically, and where they are now, it's time to have a frank discussion. My friends, it may be "un-ladylike" to focus on "business, money, and finance" (and perhaps not optimal for purposes of furthering the species), but the truth is, we live in a capitalist society. And for better or worse, in this society, money IS power.

Putting Your Wealth to Use

If all this money talk makes you feel a little squeamish, focus your thoughts on the unique and powerful position this puts women in. At this moment in time, women are in an amazing position to back other women entrepreneurs. Imagine what would happen if women decided to pool their wealth to support women-owned businesses around the world and to promote gender equality in companies. Through crowd-funding initiatives and angel investing programs, women are just beginning to wake up to the possibilities.

As exciting as these investment opportunities are, they are, unfortunately, rarely well-coordinated. Investing in single businesses is, at best, a piece-meal strategy that is not likely to have a broad impact—which means if women focus on these types of investments alone, their power and wealth will remain underutilized. However, with ESG investing, we can dump fuel on this fire by directly influencing companies, including large corporations, to enact policies that will have a broader impact, not only for women entrepreneurs but also for men and women everywhere. Instead of helping one woman or one village at a time, we can help the thousands, millions, or billions affected by corporate policies that do real harm.

Let's think bigger—what would happen, for example, if we could vote on a resolution to put pressure on corporations to make gender diversity on their boards or among C-suite leadership a top priority? In this way, women can promote gender equality from the top-down, impact cleaner environmental practices, enact better gun policies, and create better working conditions. This is real power!

Now, after reading this far, you might wonder if my true intentions in writing this book are to elevate women purely because they're women. In other words, you might think all this talk about changing the world is simply a façade disguising my radical feminism. But let me assure you, while I *am* trying to start a movement, I'm not motivated to empower women by disempowering men. I just truly believe that we all have a social responsibility to engage—to leverage our voices in creating the world we want. And I find women are less prone to leverage their voices for all the reasons we've discussed—although study after study shows women are good for business.

Involvement by women has been shown to enhance corporate profitability. For example, the McKinsey "Delivering Through Diversity" report from 2018 found that companies in the top quartile for gender diversity were 15% more likely to experience above average profitability than those in the lowest quartile.[32] Also, having greater female representation in the boardroom results in better acquisition and investment decisions and less aggressive risk-taking, all of which benefits shareholders.[33] Let's face it, if women represent 47% of the total workforce in the U.S. and are currently earning more educational degrees than men, it stands to reason that improving women's economic success is the last, best bastion of hope for increasing the nation's GDP.[34]

So, yes, I believe that a rising tide lifts all boats. When women do better, all of society does better. And yet, women are continually strapped economically by old stereotypes, old ways of thinking, the challenges of being a mom, and fears (rational or not) of financial insecurity. To reiterate, this isn't about elevating women because they're women. It's about showing women how much power they have and showing them how they can use their power to get more of what they want, including more of what will bring about positive social change for all of us.

Okay, But What Do Women Want?

Do women even want to use their money to change society? The answer is unequivocally, "Yes."

- In my Women, Wealth, and ESG Study, 95% of women (55-75, with more than $500,000 in assets) reported giving at least $100 annually to charity and 36% reported giving more than $1,000.

- Women of all ages give in larger numbers to philanthropy than men: 64% of donations are made by women.[35]

- Women volunteer at higher rates (28%) than men (22%).[36]

- 84% of women report interest in "sustainable" investing—that is focusing on financial as well as social and environmental goals. The figure for men is 67%.[37] (*I should note here that 80% of the boomer women participating in my survey reported being unfamiliar with sustainable investing, so I find this statistic difficult to square with my research. I discuss possible reasons for this discrepancy in a later chapter.*)

Yet, my anecdotal experience, confirmed by various outside research sources, shows that there is a significant gap between women's motivations and their actions as it relates to putting their money where their mouths are. A 2017 survey conducted by Morgan Stanley's Institute for Sustainable Investment found that while 84% of women report interest in sustainable investing, only 40% report having actually incorporated sustainability into their investment decisions.[38] And even though the number of individual women outpaces men when it comes to donating to causes they care about, women generally give in smaller quantities than their male counterparts. For example, as the chart below shows, a record number of women donated to Hillary Clinton's presidential campaign. However, men still gave the most money and were the largest individual donors.[39] Again, I attribute these types of discrepancies to women's fears of outliving their assets.

Women are also generally more timid about exerting power and influence, perhaps having been socialized to believe that the pursuit of either (or both) is, yet again, "un-ladylike." These underlying cultural attitudes result in women, for example, being more likely to give anonymously, while men are more likely to demand naming rights for the new hospital wing they funded. Unfortunately, however, women's timid behavior surrounding the pursuit of money and its influence has led to a huge power gap, with women taking the backseat.

Now that we're convinced that collectively women have untapped power to access wealth and bring about social change, why is ESG the right vehicle to bring about change?

Why ESG?

Fortunately, there is now a new way to throw the power of your wealth behind issues you care about. It doesn't require that you give more of your money away or that you put your financial future in jeopardy to make a difference. Nor does it require you to make your contributions public (though you really should see what it feels like to have your name on a building).

I referenced it above, but for the sake of clarity, let's discuss it again. It is called ESG investing and it incorporates a dual mandate that allows you to invest your wealth for the purpose of earning a financial return (yes, you continue to build your nest egg), while simultaneously impacting the causes you care about. With the availability of ESG, you no longer must choose between doing good and doing what's in your financial best interest. You don't have to give up all your worldly possessions and go on a mission trip or join the Peace Corps (not that there's anything wrong with doing these types of things) to make the world a better place. For the first time, you have attractive options to help you do good in the world while also improving your personal financial situation.

As in the gun example with Dick's Sporting Goods and Walmart that started us down this path, you can join a social media movement to boycott and/or divest from companies whose policies you want to protest. Or, what may turn out to be even more impactful over the long term—you can influence the behavior of companies you wish to change by *buying* their stocks and voting on shareholder resolutions that demand change. Investing with an ESG lens allows you to join forces with other investors to make a real difference. While it's difficult to influence behavior as a single investor, when acting in concert with a group of other like-minded investors and using your collective power to amplify your single voice, real change is possible.

If you're skeptical about corporate ability to influence social change, consider this statement per *As You Sow*, a shareholder advocacy group:[40]

"Over the past century, corporate power has become the most dominant force on the planet. Of the 100 largest economic entities in the world, nearly 70% are corporations. This concentration of resources gives companies power and influence over their workers, customers, and the communities in which they operate."

And if have doubts about the ability of shareholders to influence gigantic corporations, remember the power of the almighty dollar is absolutely paramount. You may be surprised at how much companies take notice when even 10% of their shareholders sign onto a resolution urging a policy change. In most of these cases, businesses will take the path of least resistance which is often giving the people what they want. Around 45% of all corporate resolutions were withdrawn in 2018 indicating that companies were changing their policies almost half the time, even before such resolutions made it to a vote.[41] I have much more to say about how ESG-factor investing works and how you can get involved in later chapters.

NOW is the Time to Act

There's only one more question left to answer in this chapter: *Why now?*

I began to answer this question in the Introduction. Boomer women have more wealth than any other generation of women in U.S. history which means we have more power and potential influence now than ever before. If we don't put our wealth to work, we will squander perhaps the best opportunity we've ever had to bring about meaningful change. History has also shown us that the window of time to take advantage of this opportunity will close quickly.

But beyond this, there is a growing hunger for social change, while at the same time, a growing dissatisfaction with the traditional methods of enacting change. Recall that less than 30% of respondents in my survey expressed confidence in the ability of the U.S. political system to solve our social problems, which aligns with a recent Gallup poll showing that only 34% of Americans in general are satisfied with our political system and its efficacy.[42]

Before you jump to conclusions about this administration or that administration, note that the Gallup number has remained relatively unchanged since 2011 defying attempts to pin the blame on one political party over another. In this day and age, where more than half the country feels politically disenfranchised (no matter which party is in charge), political gridlock frustrates efforts toward meaningful progress, and change—real change—happens far too slowly, ESG investing holds the promise of a more direct route to exerting influence.

So, while the concept of exerting economic pressure to influence change is nothing new, there is one final factor which makes *now* the time for women investors to align their values with their portfolios. Up until only recently, values-based investing has come at a financial cost. Fewer investment options coupled with higher fees meant that investment returns suffered relative to a standard portfolio. However, as the demand for ESG-factor investing has grown, led primarily by institutional investors such as large pension funds and endowments, more and more options have become available at lower price points such that today you can align your portfolio with your values while earning comparable (and some argue, better) returns. This means that taking collective action is more accessible to the average investor than ever before.

Yes, you now can use your investments to do good while continuing to do well for yourself and your family. Yes, this approach is easier, takes less time, and is arguably more effective than political and philanthropic means of enacting change. But it also requires a bit of strategy. If making a difference with your investment dollars is something that interests you, it's essential to educate yourself about the options. I've already explained why I think you should give ESG investing serious consideration. Throughout the remainder of this book, I'll convince you that incorporating these investment criteria into your portfolio is not only good for society at large, it's also good for women *en masse*. The best part is that it's good for your bottom line, too.

So, what is wealth, you ask again? Well, in my book (no pun intended), if you can exert influence while increasing your wealth, you've discovered what it means to be truly "rich."

CHAPTER 2

Values-Based Investing:
A Dual Mandate

Ask any investor what her portfolio did last year, and you might hear something like "My returns were in line with the market," or "I did great!" A more engaged investor may be able to relay how her performance fared relative to a given benchmark. For example, "The stock market was up 10%, and my account did a bit better." But rephrase this question to ask, "What causes did you support with your investment dollars last year?" and you will likely be met with a blank stare. Not only do few average investors know what stocks and bonds they own, they also don't tend to think of their investments as "supporting particular causes." It is somewhat shocking (let me reiterate, *shocking*) that the power of the investment dollar has been so politically underutilized in this country—underutilized by ordinary citizens, that is. After all, we do live in a capitalist society where money motivates virtually every action.

And yet, when it comes to exerting social or political influence, the first ideas that come to mind are donating to the presidential candidate of your choice (as an aside, it should be noted that women are becoming politically engaged in the 2020 presidential election at an earlier point than ever before in history. More than 1 million women have donated to 2020 candidates so far[43]), texting your local representatives, attending a political rally, doing volunteer work, or donating money to your favorite charity. While these actions are thoughtful and generous, there are quite frankly few among us who have enough time or money to move the needle on causes we care about using these traditional methods alone.

By contrast, ESG investing has the potential to redefine how we see our wealth and our ability to use our wealth to support our values. For example, if your biggest social concern is climate change, you can influence the behavior of the largest corporations with the most significant potential impact to our planet by using your proxy voting power to support policy proposals, along with other shareholders, that align with your views about the environment. Similarly, if your primary social concern is gender inequality in the C-suite, you can choose to invest in companies that promote and support women leaders or better yet, invest in a fund with a manager specifically committed to *influencing* companies to support more gender equality. Being removed from an investment fund poses a great economic risk for companies, so many companies will bow to pressure from fund managers who can act on behalf of shareholders. In addition to your ballot and your donations, using ESG investment criteria gives you the power to put the full weight of your investment dollars behind the causes you care about.

But I'm jumping ahead a bit. To really understand how ESG can work for you, we've first got to know a bit about the history of values-based investing.

A Brief History of Values-Based Investing

'ESG' was first coined as a term of art among financial professionals in 2005,[44] but the concept of "doing good while doing well" is certainly nothing new. We can trace this dual mandate concept back at least to 17th-century England when the Quakers first articulated the "blended value vision of faith, commerce, and community." Although Americans associate Quakers with oatmeal, when this group of Christians crossed the Atlantic and landed in Philadelphia, they planted the seeds of America's own Industrial Revolution. Bethlehem Steel was founded by Joseph Wharton, a Quaker entrepreneur, who also endowed the first collegiate business school at the University of Pennsylvania—the Wharton School. In addition to their business influence, the Quakers were ahead of their time on social issues. As a group, they prohibited participation in the slave trade in 1758—more than a century prior to Lincoln issuing the Emancipation Proclamation.

Later, John Wesley, a preacher and the founder of Methodism, was among the most vocal adopters of the dual mandate philosophy. In a famous sermon on money given in 1786, Wesley stressed that Christians should not harm their neighbors in the pursuit of their business interests. Putting his words into action, he warned against industries and practices that could harm workers and urged his congregants not to put their money into "sinful" companies, such as those associated with liquor, tobacco, and guns—what are today referred to as the "sin stocks."[45] In a moment, we'll see this type of "negative screen" investment strategy labeled as *Socially Responsible Investing*.

The dual-mandate movement was relatively quiet for nearly 200 years. Unsurprisingly, however, the renewed focus on individual freedom and civil rights in the 1960s breathed new life into the evolution of the dual mandate philosophy. Socially concerned investors sought to address equality for women, civil rights, human rights, and labor issues.

Most notably, outrage over napalm use during the Vietnam War resulted in a direct backlash against Dow Chemical, the producer of napalm. Amidst student protests and citizen-organized boycotts, colleges, religious organizations, and other institutions divested of Dow stock. In January 1969, the Union Theological Seminary divested itself of 6,000 shares because they believed that Dow symbolized "a kind of warfare that is morally repellent [sic]."[46]

On the heels of the highly charged 1960s, the PAX World Fund (the first socially responsible mutual fund in the U.S.) was created. This fund focused on challenging corporations to live up to specific social and environmental standards including preventing the production of nuclear weapons.

More recently and what has perhaps been the most powerful iteration of this theme was the economic divestment of South Africa during the anti-apartheid movement. Here again, American student protesters pressured colleges to divest their endowments of companies doing business in South Africa. By 1988, a total of 155 U.S. colleges had at least partially divested. While divestment started with colleges, other large institutions also followed suit. From 1985 to 1990, over 200 U.S. companies cut ties with South Africa resulting in a $1 billion loss of direct investment. The divestment movement had an obvious and dramatic impact on the South African economy and ultimately, real change was achieved, the culmination of which was the democratic election of Nelson Mandela in 1994.

The history of values-based investing is full of lessons for individual investors interested in the ESG movement today. The wins have been hard fought and at times seem to have moved with glacial speed. But we cannot assume the same methods of exerting economic pressure to influence behavior will work in every situation, as the effectiveness of different strategies is highly dependent upon context. The Napalm example is a case of a divestment strategy combined with public boycotts. This approach worked at the time largely because Napalm was primarily used as a military weapon. In other words, the world could live without napalm. But would the same strategy be as effective today with fossil fuels?

And in the 1980s, countries with the most economic power could afford not to do business with South Africa. But suppose there was a movement in the U.S. today to stop doing business with China in support of the Hong Kong protestors. Would this divestment strategy be realistic? Even if it were, would it work in the same way it did with the anti-apartheid movement? These are important questions to ask.

My point is that while ESG has its roots in socially responsible investing, I believe ESG is the dual mandate philosophy for modern times, as it offers more flexibility and potentially more influence over the policies you wish to change. In addition, you can expect similar returns as that of an unconstrained portfolio. For now, the main point is that you'll need to consider the strategies that work best given the specific issues you are trying to address. I'll talk more specifically about how ESG works for today's investor and why I recommend this values-based strategy above others shortly.

Let's first clarify the many terms that have been used to describe dual mandate investing since these terms are often used interchangeably and inappropriately. For example, what's the difference between Values-Based Investing (VBI), Impact Investing (II), Socially Responsible Investing (SRI), Sustainable Investing (SI), and ESG (Environmental, Social, and Governance) factor investing? Let's make some distinctions for the sake of clarification, keeping in mind, however, that there are no hard and fast rules determining which is the "right" terminology.

Values-Based Investing (VBI)

This broad term describes any kind of investment strategy that incorporates not only the growth potential of the investment, but the values of the investor. This is where the dual mandate philosophy comes in: doing well (financially) while also doing good in the world. It includes all the types of investing listed below, though each of these varies in focus, objective, and degree.

Impact Investing (II)

Impact investing is used most often to describe a *private* investment in any project or program designed to accomplish a specific goal that benefits society. Generally, these investments are outside the purview of the public markets. In other words, impact investing cannot be achieved by buying public stocks or bonds; rather, impact investing involves a special private project. For example, starting a school in South Africa and hoping to create a self-sustaining model would be a form of impact investing.

Note also that while impact investors want to see a positive financial return, many are willing to take on more risk and accept lower returns in exchange for creating positive social change. So, while this type of values-based investing does include a dual mandate, the focus is on the social impact—more so than the financial return. Again, this type of investing is typically made by higher net worth individuals who can "afford" lower financial returns.

Socially Responsible Investing (SRI)

SRI, on the other hand, looks more like a traditional stock portfolio, but is most commonly associated with eliminating (or screening out) companies whose activities run counter to the values of an investor. Some common examples of negative screening may include eliminating companies promoting "sin stocks" such as military weapons, tobacco, alcohol, and abortion, though any investment considered misaligned with the investor's personal ethics may be excluded.

When college endowments in the late 1960s divested of Dow Chemical stocks as a way to voice their opposition to Napalm, they were using a negative screen. The major drawback to this type of values-based investing is that entire sectors of the market may be eliminated or over-concentrated depending on an investor's values, potentially reducing both the diversification of a portfolio (thereby increasing risk) and its returns. In addition, as we'll learn later, eliminating the stocks of companies whose policies you don't like actually takes away any sense of control you might have over the company. You can no longer vote on their board resolutions; you can no longer be part of a shareholder resolution. In other words, you lose the ability to be a shareholder activist.

Environmental, Social, and Governance (ESG)

ESG investing (a term often used interchangeably with *Sustainable Investing*) builds on the concept of SRI but recognizes that the ESG behaviors of companies can impact investment returns both positively and negatively. As such, ESG investing seeks to build a values-based portfolio that also generates strong, positive returns for investors. This is the *only* values-based investment strategy that treats both sides of the dual mandate as equally important.

Starting with a carefully constructed traditional portfolio designed to meet the financial risk and return goals of the investor, ESG investing includes an additional criterion (or factor) related to a company's Environmental, Social, and Governance policies. While reputational risk has always been a consideration for traditional portfolio construction, ESG offers a more systemized approach in selecting companies that meet specific ESG criteria while also meeting the traditional risk and reward criteria for the investment. This gives ESG investing a distinct advantage over other forms of values-based investing.

For example, if carbon emissions are an important issue for the investor, rather than divesting all energy stocks (as one might in an SRI approach), the investor would select funds that include energy companies moving toward better and more sustainable practices, such as pledging not to use fracking techniques and/or investing in wind and solar projects. In this way, investors can actively influence corporate behavior toward a more sustainable approach. And since ESG includes all asset classes, optimal diversification is maintained which is key to reducing financial risk. This is why I believe ESG is a true dual mandate option and the reason I recommend it to any values-based investor who is equally interested in achieving market-like returns.

How Does ESG Work?

When I think of ESG investing, I think of Donald Trump. You might laugh or roll your eyes but hear me out. Whatever your political leanings and whatever you think about Trump himself, it's hard to deny that the man has remarkably learned how to bypass the media and the gridlock of Washington, at least when it comes to putting his uncensored point of view out there. In other words, through his tweets, Trump directly communicates with his constituency, the American public, and the world in a completely unfiltered way. While you may or may not appreciate Trump's ability to move entire world markets with a single push of a button (I might argue that we need better guidelines surrounding *anyone's* ability to move world markets with a single push of a button), the fact remains that he has found an effective, direct route to influence world events.

Similarly, values-based investing, using ESG principles in particular, can bypass gridlock in Washington by going directly to the companies whose policies you wish to change. No more waiting for your politician to do what he promised. No more waiting another four years until a presidential election can swing the pendulum on issues you care about. You can "vote" every day with your investment dollars.

Let's take a closer look at what ESG investing can do. If you want to use your investment dollars to impact social causes, such as reducing carbon emissions, reducing access to assault-style weapons, and increasing the number of women in corporate leadership, you can use a variety of ESG tools to help you make investment decisions in line with your beliefs. You can focus on portfolio construction which is a more passive approach to values-based investing, active ownership, or any combination of the two:[47]

Portfolio Construction (Passive Ownership)

As an investor, you can use your portfolio to influence change simply through what and how much of a specific company or industry you hold in your portfolio. Portfolio construction is a passive ownership approach because you are not actively engaging with either the boards or management teams of the companies within your portfolio. There are two ways to use this method:

1. *ESG Integration*: Sometimes referred to as "best in class," this method means you choose funds or companies with the best ESG ratings from all industry sectors when constructing your portfolio. The companies with higher ESG ratings are over-represented in the portfolio, while the lower ESG scoring companies are underrepresented. This weighting system sends an indirect message to companies: *If you want a higher representation within the portfolio or fund, you will need to change your behavior.* This option is the most likely to provide financial returns similar to a non-ESG focused portfolio.

2. *Negative/Positive Screens*: As an alternative, you may decide to completely eliminate certain industries you don't want to support such as gun manufacturing, fossil fuels, and the like. Or you may decide to only own certain sectors/industries. Your portfolio will be constructed to exclude and/or include only the industries you've specified, resulting in a different risk/return profile than a non-constrained portfolio. This method is more appropriately termed socially responsible investing (SRI), as opposed to ESG investing. As we've discussed before, the social benefit of this method will greatly depend on context.

Shareholder Advocacy (Active Ownership)

As an investor, you can also intentionally own companies within your portfolio whose behaviors you hope to change. You can influence company behavior using one or both of the methods below.

1. *Proxy Voting:* Active ownership allows you to intentionally purchase stocks of companies whose behavior you want to change or influence. By owning these companies, you now can vote on *company* resolutions by proxy. Resolutions give you the opportunity to vote for or against issues proposed by the company's *management* and *board*. Note that a proxy vote is a ballet cast by an individual or a firm on behalf of a shareholder who is unable to attend the annual shareholder meeting. Proxy voting season comes along each spring when publicly traded companies report their activities to shareholders during their annual meetings. Prior to these meetings, shareholders receive information relevant to the topics up for vote such as share ownership, the structure of the board of directors, or executive compensation. Investors can discuss their voting preferences with their money managers or fund managers and come up with a strategy for influencing corporate behavior in alignment with their personal values.

2. *Shareholder Resolutions:* If you want to be even more engaged, you can bring new issues to the company by joining with other like-minded investors to file *shareholder* resolutions.[48] Shareholder resolutions are a powerful way to get your voice heard as they can directly encourage corporate responsibility and discourage unsustainable, unethical, or risky policies. Resolutions to be filed appear in the company's proxy statement and all shareholders have an opportunity to see and vote on them. In this way, shareholder resolutions open a line of communication between shareholders and management that often results in changes in company policy. You'll see a case study on this shortly.

As you can see, obtaining accurate information about company behavior is the vital first step in employing any of the above strategies. So how do shareholders get their hands on ESG information about the companies they own? Today, most large publicly traded corporations publish reports on their ESG initiatives (think Facebook, Starbucks, Amazon, and Apple)[49] that can be used to help investors evaluate the policies of these companies. If you're thinking that self-reporting may be biased and not the most effective way for investors to get the information they need to make good investment decisions, you're not alone.

As a result, a third-party ratings system similar to the credit rating system for ESG factors has evolved. Historically, ESG ratings were provided by index providers such as MSCI and a few specialty firms such as Sustainalytics. However, we now have over 100 ratings agencies doing this work. Note that although the ESG rating system is relatively new with plenty of room for improved standardization and oversight, it provides a good starting point for evaluating sustainability issues as it relates to public companies.

In addition, the U.S. Federal Government and the U.N. are both encouraging all major credit rating agencies to offer ESG rankings specific to bonds. Moody's and S&P Global Ratings are the latest to announce they will include ESG sections in their corporate credit rating reports, adding another layer of analysis to the public bond industry.[50]

Let's now demystify the term ESG. Analysts rate companies on each of the following three categories:

Environmental Issues

Environmental factors include ways in which a company uses energy, contributes to climate change, releases carbon emissions, manages pollution, treats animals, uses land, and conserves natural resources, among other factors. This metric can also measure how a company is managing environmental risk including its handling of hazardous waste and toxic emissions. Finally, it includes a company's compliance with environmental regulations.

Note that a company's negative environmental impact can also have a direct negative impact on its financial performance. Take the Volkswagen scandal as an example. In September of 2015, we learned Volkswagen had intentionally programmed its emissions control system to activate only during emissions testing. During normal driving conditions, however, emissions were actually 40 times the amount found during testing. This software—designed to cheat regulators—resulted not only in environmental damage, but also did considerable financial harm, costing the company $33 billion and counting.[51] Obviously, the stock price suffered (i.e., the shareholder) as did the brand.

Social Issues

Social factors encompass the ways in which a company interacts with other businesses and the broader community. Does the company treat its employees well? Is the company a good corporate citizen? Does the company have honorable labor practices? Social factors can also include hiring and labor practices such as gender and ethnic diversity, human rights, and consumer protection policies.

You may recall the 2017 United Airlines scandal when the company suffered a $1 billion loss after a video showing two security guards dragging a passenger off an overbooked flight went viral. The non-apology from CEO Oscar Munoz stated that while he was "upset" by the incident, United employees were simply following company protocols and procedures. The CEO's response created a PR nightmare for United, but the issue of overbooking flights went much deeper. Ultimately, United Airlines changed its policy such that a passenger cannot be removed from a flight to accommodate a crew member.[52] This change did not perhaps go far enough to satisfy the public, but it was at least an indication that United was listening.

As this example shows, identifying companies with questiona-ble social policies and practices will not only incentivize companies to more closely evaluate their behaviors, but it will allow investors to make preemptive judgments about whether to invest. Ideally, a closer look at social factors will prevent investors from getting in-volved with companies having poor practices surrounding the treatment of their customers. Making information about ESG be-havior more widely available promises to make corporations bet-ter, while rewarding investors for being attentive to more than their bottom lines.

Governance Issues

Corporate governance refers to the ways in which a company inter-acts with its primary stakeholders, including its shareholders and employees. Is the company transparent in its accounting practices? Does the company take proper precautions to avoid conflicts of in-terest? Does the board represent the interests of *all* stakeholders in terms of its diversity and structure?

Studies show that governance factors impacting company cul-ture can also impact a company's financial performance. In fact, some have argued that the root cause of the emissions scandal at Volkswagen was actually broken corporate governance which put pressure on managers to achieve unrealistic goals. The same could be said about the Wells Fargo scandal that resulted in accounts be-ing opened for customers without their knowledge. All of this shows that issues related to corporate governance are extremely important as the culture at the top tends to trickle down.

What about gender equality? Yes, this is a governance issue and an area that is especially important for women, but also for all share-holders, since studies show that women can potentially enhance de-cision making and therefore can potentially enhance profits for all investors. One group of researchers found that firms with female directors had less aggressive investment policies, made better acquisition decisions, and saw improved financial performance, especially in industries with a tendency toward overconfidence among leaders.[53] As with environmental factors and social factors, there are good reasons to be optimistic about corporate governance ratings correlating with higher returns for investors.

Below is a more inclusive summary of the three different areas covered by ESG:[54]

1. **Environmental**

   - Waste and Pollution
   - Resource Depletion
   - Greenhouse Gas Emission
   - Deforestation
   - Climate Change

2. **Social**

   - Employee Relations and Diversity
   - Working Conditions, Including Child Labor and Slavery
   - Local Communities; Seeks Explicitly to Fund Projects or Institutions That Will Serve Poor and Underserved Communities Globally
   - Health and Safety
   - Conflict

3. **Governance**

   - Tax Strategy
   - Executive Remuneration
   - Donations and Political Lobbying
   - Corruption and Bribery
   - Board Diversity and Structure

Example: Taking Climate Change Seriously With ESG

Now that you better understand the kinds of issues that can be addressed through values-based investing, we need to discuss specific ways you can get involved and utilize your investments. Let's say your portfolio is worth $500k and you're extremely conscientious about climate change. You care deeply about the environment and worry daily about leaving your children with such a huge mess to clean up. Perhaps you don't feel that either the political system or non-profit corporations are attacking this issue with the urgency it deserves. Perhaps you feel disenfranchised, disempowered, and helpless to make a difference when it comes to this issue you care about so deeply.

Then, you read this book (apologies for the shameless self-promotion) and a lightbulb goes off. You realize you can align your portfolio with your desire to make a difference on environmental issues. You then decide to invest in a more climate friendly portfolio.

You have a few options:

Negative Screen

You can decide you won't invest in any energy companies utilizing fossil fuels and divest of these holdings in your portfolio. This investment strategy is most closely associated with SRI investing (see above). Be aware that if you go this route—that is, eliminating any stock with ties to the fossil fuel industry—you may see a reduction in your investment returns over the long term given our world's current reliance on fossil fuels. The negative screening route can also lead to increased risk as it will likely decrease the diversification of your portfolio.

A bigger drawback to going with a negative screening approach, however, is that you may not actually have the impact you hope to achieve. Sure, divesting of fossil fuels might make you feel more socially responsible and relieve you of some guilty feelings, but will it cause companies to change their behavior? Very unlikely. Consider how many stocks are traded in a single day on the U.S. stock exchange. In 2017, an average of 6.43 billion shares were traded per day and that was a "down" year for trading volatility.[55] Selling off your shares will go entirely unnoticed, and even if you happen to be part of a wave of sell offs that cause fossil fuel companies to take notice, they may not make the connection between shareholders' values and company policies. Perhaps the sales are due to normal portfolio rebalancing. Or because the company's stock has become overvalued. These reasons have nothing to do with the ESG behaviors of the company. Remember, too, that by definition, when you sell your shares, someone else is buying them. Does this really send a message to the company?

Positive Screen

Alternatively, you can decide to invest only in wind, solar, and other "clean energy" companies. You could use this strategy in addition to the negative screen, replacing fossil fuel reliant companies with "clean energy" stocks and funds. Or you could use this strategy on its own as a criterion for future investments. In this case, you might leave your current portfolio mostly unchanged, but as you add to your portfolio in the future using your current investment strategy, you may use specific environmental factors to invest in funds with good ESG ratings, especially those committed to improving environmental conditions.

Notice here again, though, in terms of impact, using a positive screen is no better than using a negative screen. Your ability as an individual investor to bring about change by buying certain stocks and funds is similar to your ability as an individual consumer to bring about change by choosing to shop at certain retailers. Again, given the volume of stocks being traded every day, individual investors cannot make much of an impact buying or selling stocks on their own.

ESG Integration

Another alternative is to invest only in financially promising energy companies that are currently utilizing fossil fuels and are also developing alternative forms of energy such as wind and solar farms. Or those energy companies that are being more environmentally conscious in their drilling activities. In other words, you're investing in all asset classes, but only in those companies that are the most sustainably focused. This "best in class" strategy is the one I recommend most often when I discuss ESG criteria with my clients.

A small, but mighty group of fund managers (like Parametric, who you'll learn more about below) is committed to offering investment solutions with an eye toward enacting real social change. These fund managers purchase company stocks that not only have high ESG ratings, but those that have also shown a willingness to listen to shareholder concerns. By investing in this category of funds, shareholders can make a real difference and be involved in pushing corporations to make changes aligned with their values.

In addition to adjusting their portfolios in alignment with their values, shareholders can take collective action through proxy voting and shareholder resolutions to push policy changes with companies that have already demonstrated a willingness to make values-based changes. And they can do so without risking their own financial legacies because they're investing in stocks that rank well both in terms of likely returns and in terms of doing good in the world. Again, this is the option that best honors both sides of the dual mandate strategy.

ESG investing is a great way to get involved with the climate change movement and potentially become an activist shareholder, but you're probably (and rightfully) also concerned about outliving your assets (recall the "bag lady" syndrome).

Is ESG Really a Smart Way to Invest?

This all sounds great, you say. But is ESG investing actually smart investing? Can you really make a difference on climate change (or other ESG issues) without sacrificing your financial wellbeing? It's true that had you wanted to practice socially responsible investing prior to 2005, when negative screens were the only option, it likely would have required you to sacrifice something in terms of the returns on your investments. Back then, values-based investing was a niche investment strategy available only to the wealthiest philanthropists and huge institutional investors like colleges and universities. But today with governments, regulators, and the general public paying more attention (thank you, social media) to ESG factors, there's good reason to believe companies with strong records on ESG are actually *better* investments than those that do not focus on social responsibility.

Also, it stands to reason that if you're not eliminating entire sectors of the public market from your portfolio, but rather selecting only those companies with better ESG mandates, you could expect your portfolio might actually perform better in the long run. As public demand rises for companies to pay attention to more than profits, markets will reward companies that follow suit. In other words, part of the value proposition when investing with an ESG mandate is that good corporate governance and behavior will reduce the risk of an eventual decline in share value, or worse, complete obsolescence. So, ESG standards can be thought of as another layer of due diligence for investors.

But you don't have to take my word for it. Let's look at the data. A study conducted took the return results of four different portfolios: the "unconstrained" portfolio made up of every stock in the S&P 500 index, an SRI portfolio (negative/positive screens of entire sectors), an ESG portfolio (best in class of every sector), and a portfolio with combined SRI and ESG constraints.

While no sample is full-proof, the study showed that ESG invest-ing outperformed the other three portfolios by .09% per year over a five-year period (October of 2004-November of 2009, incorporat-ing the financial downturn of 2008) and outperformed four out of five years on a risk-adjusted basis.[56]

The differential may not seem big, but at a minimum, it demon-strates that ESG investing does not result in lower returns. At best, it demonstrates that ESG investing can boost long-term performance.

Another review of over 2,200 independent *studies* shows that the integration of ESG into portfolios had either a neutral or positive relationship to performance 90% of the time, across asset classes, over time.[57] That is to say, 90% of the time, investing in an ESG port-folio produced either the same results or better results than a tradi-tional portfolio.

Fortunately, ESG is no longer a separate allocation or "carve out," nor is it any longer considered a "niche" field. Interest in ESG has now become mainstream with over $12 trillion of assets profession-ally managed utilizing ESG, a 50% increase since 2016 alone.[58] In fact, 26% of all professionally managed assets are invested in socially re-sponsible investments of one type or another with 74% of these coming from institutional investors and 26% coming from money managers on behalf of individual investors.

To be fair, there are critics. Some argue that ESG is simply a mar-keting gimmick, a "greenwashing" tactic—a trend where compa-nies find a way to claim they are environmentally friendly in their marketing materials solely to capitalize on the public outcry for "green" products—designed to attract new investors, particularly women and millennials. Others argue that the criteria used to de-fine an ESG portfolio are inconsistent and vague, resulting in unre-liable outcomes.

While it's true that the criteria used to create ESG rankings have yet to be standardized, there are reasons to be optimistic here. With the number of ratings agencies exceeding 100 and the largest credit ratings agencies with the longest track records (e.g., Moody's and S&P Global) getting involved, the amount of public scrutiny in these areas will only grow over time. Certainly, shining a light on sustainable practices will motivate more standardization across the ESG ratings industry.

As I always tell my clients, do your own research and decide what's best for you. However, if you encounter critics of values based and ESG investing, be sure to scrutinize the evidence carefully. Often those who come out most strongly against these practices point to older studies when the dual mandate proposition was in its nascent stage.

As noted previously, in the early years, the only option for investors was the negative screen option when entire market sectors were excluded from portfolios. At that time, ESG funds were less accessible to the average investor and consequently more expensive, so it's not surprising that returns suffered. Further, those willing to accept lower returns were viewed as "tree hugging" extremists—not financially savvy investors, though perhaps their hearts were in the right place.

So, critics of ESG are often comparing apples to oranges. However, all signs indicate these perceptions are shifting in ways that are favorable to ESG. The demand for ESG by institutional funds, changing demographics, and improved technology has broadened the landscape and refined the concept such that today investors can earn comparable returns while also using their wealth to influence the world. If your perception of ESG is clouded by earlier iterations of this investment strategy, it may be time to reconsider.

Key Takeaway:

Ladies, I'm aware of the technical nature of this chapter. Having worked with hundreds of women investors, I recognize that learning the ins and outs of investing may not be your number one priority. I'm not asking you to become an investment expert. I'm not even asking you to manage your own portfolio (but certainly do this if you prefer). I *am* asking you, however, to consider the following fact: although women control the majority of wealth in this country, they are also more likely to leave investment *decisions* to others. This is even more perplexing given that boomer women view themselves as better investors than men!

Per my Women, Wealth, and ESG survey, only 13% of women feel men are better investors than themselves, yet, most women I know let their husbands take the lead on investment decisions.

My challenge to you, therefore, is to take control of your wealth and make a difference with your investment dollars. This doesn't mean you have to do it alone. By all means, use a financial advisor if you prefer. What it does mean is that you—and only *you*—should direct how you want your assets managed. *You* should decide what risk level is appropriate for you; *you* should decide whether you want an ESG portfolio; *you* should determine who your advisor is (if you utilize one); *you* should know your net worth. Don't let anyone take this power away from you. Use the power and influence that is at your fingertips. If each of you will do this, our collective voices will be heard, and real change will be achievable.

In the next chapter, we'll look at the survey results which identifies the things we have in common, the causes we collectively care about, and the way we view ourselves and our wealth. Sometimes the results are shocking (e.g., that women think of themselves as better investors than men). Other times, the results were as expected. In each case, however, the results from this survey have given me great insight into how we can collectively work together on our most pressing social problems. Understanding these insights will help you direct your investing strategy in a way that aligns with your values.

CHAPTER 3

Women and Values-Based Investing—A Recipe for Social Change

As a woman working with women and as a mother of a daughter, you don't have to tell me that women are complex. We can't be generalized. We can obviously have vastly different views on the same topic. But if we want to have the greatest impact at a time when we have the greatest voting power (and in case I haven't been crystal clear so far, I'm talking about voting with our investment dollars here), we need to stand together. It seems reasonable to assume that if women vote "together" while controlling the majority of the nation's wealth, a real opportunity to create change exists.

In this chapter, I provide you with a summary of the key findings from my Women, Wealth, and ESG study—how boomer women view themselves, the world, and the social issues they most care about. If, after reviewing this section, you feel that you would benefit from a deeper dive, please refer to Appendix A for the complete survey results and methodology utilized.

Key Findings and Insights:

1. Regardless of political affiliation, we women have a lot in common.

Given how divided the country feels, I find it especially affirming to know that regardless of political affiliation, boomer women generally view themselves and their wealth similarly. In my survey, 38% identified as Democrat, 35% as Republican, 18% Independent, and 9% stated that they do not have any political affiliation or preferred not to answer. In spite of these differences, it's clear that the boomer women surveyed are all generally frustrated with the lack of social progress and would welcome an opportunity to use their investment dollars to exert influence over the causes they care about most deeply if given the opportunity.

2. Boomer women vastly underestimate the percentage of the nation's wealth they control.

As I have previously pointed out, women currently control somewhere between 51%-60% of the nation's wealth, and studies suggest they will control up to 67% of this wealth by 2030. This is due primarily to spousal inheritances as boomer men, with their shorter life expectancies, leave millions of dollars to their wives. However, when asked to estimate how much wealth women control, on average, respondents believed women controlled only 36% of the nation's wealth. The responses here show that even while women have made significant financial strides in terms of circumventing the wage gap, climbing the corporate ladder, starting businesses, and owning wealth, the perception about what they own continues to lag the facts.

What we might call the "perception gap" has serious consequences. Clearly, if women don't believe they have enough wealth to make a difference, they won't wield their influence. As long as women hold back and shy away from their financial power, not only do they leave money on the proverbial table, they give up their seat at the table when it comes to having a say in how our world is being shaped. Understanding the magnitude of wealth women control and the power that comes with it is the first step toward closing this gap. Understanding effective ways to wield that power is the next, most important step.

3. Women see themselves as more prudent investors of their wealth than men.

I was surprised by this finding as the perception "out there" seems to be that men are better investors than women. However, the women participating in my survey actually consider themselves to be more prudent investors than men.

The facts, referenced earlier, support the perceptions of my survey respondents too, as women, on average, earn 1.2% or more than men per year when investing.[59] This is because women tend to choose more diverse portfolios and tend to view themselves as long-term investors, while men are more likely to invest in riskier stocks, trade more often, and hold onto losing stocks longer than their female counterparts.[60] However, women also consider themselves more risk-averse than men, even though studies show that women are *not* more risk averse, but that men are over-confident[61] — hence, their lagging returns.

These responses, as well as the perception that women control just over one-third of the nation's wealth, align with my observation that few women *feel* rich. When you earn less than your male colleagues, when you're told investing and finance is a "man's game," and when only one in five financial advisors is a woman,[62] it's no wonder women don't realize their potential power.

The "perception" gap has far-reaching implications too. One poll asking Americans what they would do with an extra $1,000 found that men are 35% more likely than women to invest the extra money.[63] This explains why so much ink has been spilled about how women are less likely than men to invest in the stock market.[64] It's time, in my view, for women to step up with their investment dollars, not only in earning financial returns but in advancing social causes. My strong hope is that this book will raise awareness about the incredible power available to us. It's time to vote with our pocketbooks.

4. Most boomer women are unfamiliar with ESG (or SI)

Although, as a nation, we have seen soaring interest in sustainable investing, with figures regularly cited that over 80% of women and 90% of millennials are interested in ESG,[65] my survey suggests that 62% of boomer women of "wealth" are completely unfamiliar with ESG while another 19% report they have heard of this concept, but don't know much about it. This means that over 80% of those holding the greatest wealth in this country don't really know what ESG is. In fact, only 3% reported investing with an ESG mandate or using SI criteria.

I was so taken aback by the disparity between women's widely-reported interest in ESG and what my survey revealed that I spoke with Meg Voorhes, Director of Research at US SIF: The Forum for Sustainable and Responsible Investment.[66] She and I came up with several theories to explain the gap. One theory is that there is a generational gap that has been underreported. Perhaps the 80% statistic is being driven by younger women, but in our age group where the money is, very few know about ESG.

Another theory is that there could be a disparity between ESG interest among single women and married women. Given the majority of my participants reported being married (75%), it's possible these women are allowing their male partners to take the lead on investment decisions. And since it appears boomer men are less interested in investing for reasons beyond increasing financial returns, it stands to reason that married boomer women may not be privy to newer ways of investing that incorporate ESG.

Additionally, it's possible that many of the women in my survey rely on their financial advisors to tell them about new investment options. Given that only one in five advisors is a woman and women advisors are the ones leading the charge on ESG investing (53% of women advisors incorporate some form of ESG into their portfolios), that women are simply not being told about ESG by their advisors. In fact, a recent industry study found that 26% of male advisors say they are not using ESG criteria and will not consider doing so.[67] Whatever the reasons, there's simply not a lot of good education going on among the "monied" class of investors about ESG investing.

We know that when given the choice, women are more likely to take advantage of investment opportunities that propel change. So, clearly ESG is an underutilized opportunity.

5. A strong majority of boomer women believe companies (as compared to the U.S. political system or non-profits) have the power to bring about social change.

The result of my survey also show that women are searching for alternative ways to move the needle on social causes they care about. Traditionally, women have touted political reform as one way to change the world. How often do we hear our friends and acquaintances suggesting that if we really want to see a reduction in gun violence or an increase in green business practices, we need to go to the polls or text our representatives? And how confident are we that any real reform on the social issues that we care about the most will come out of our political system?

Women also generously support nonprofits and charities as they work to improve the lives of the underserved. However, many charities lack the funding they need to push back against special interest groups and stand up against powerful for-profit corporations.

It seems clear, however, that more Americans are finding ways to put pressure on corporations to bring about change. For example, several big corporations, including Walmart, CVS, and Publix in open carry states have decided to ask gun owners not to bring their guns into stores when shopping. As noted, Dicks Sporting Goods and Walmart have both agreed to take assault-style weapons off the shelves. Walmart also announced it would no longer sell ammunition for assault-style weapons. And 150 CEOs of American companies signed a letter calling on Congress to take action on guns. Much of this has come about as a result of social media engagement.

Similarly, a social movement surrounding the harmful effects of vaping has resulted in the FDA's launch of a new anti-vaping ad campaign aimed at teenagers.[68] Also, several states are testing legislation such as banning flavored cartridges, closing down vape shops, and stopping the sale of bootlegged cartridges that are being blamed for vaping-related lung illnesses.[69] Yes, apparently social pressure can also influence government agencies to take action.

The survey results also confirm these trends. When asked about their confidence in institutions and organizations, a strong majority of respondents (61%) reported being confident in the ability of public and private companies to bring about social change in the U.S. When compared with their confidence in nonprofits and charities (33%) and in the U.S. political system (28%), 61% is remarkable indeed. It's also interesting to note that of the three choices (companies, the political system, and nonprofits), women have the least amount of confidence in the U.S. political system to bring about change. Again, these responses come from women across the political spectrum.

Please don't misunderstand me. I'm not telling you to stay home on election day—not by any means. Absolutely stay engaged on all fronts! But also recognize that these findings show that we women are tired of waiting for change using conventional means. We have been paying attention long enough to know bureaucracy and red tape are not the best way to get anything done in America. So, while you're standing in line to vote and knocking on doors for your Presidential candidate of choice, it couldn't hurt to also put your investment dollars to better use.

6. The top social issues that boomer women care about do not align with the top issues money managers care about.

In my survey, I was especially interested to see what social issues American boomer women care about the most, regardless of political affiliation. My hypothesis was that there would be issues agreed upon by women across party lines—and the survey confirmed my suspicions.

The results of the survey are eye-opening. Not only did my survey reveal some important information about the social issues women as a whole are most concerned about, it also revealed that the top issues boomer women care about do not necessarily correlate with the top issues money managers care about.

According to a 2018 US SIF report, the top ESG criteria used by money managers are: [70]

1. Climate Change
2. Tobacco
3. Conflict Risk (Terrorist or Repressive Regimes)
4. Human Rights
5. Transparency and Anti-Corruption

In my survey, the top five issues that stood out (in ranked order) were as follows:

1. Ethics/moral/religious/family decline
2. Lack of gun control laws
3. Environment/pollution/climate change
4. Human rights violations
5. Wage gap between men and women

More research and analysis would need to be done to delve into what accounts for the discrepancies here. But one thing is clear, if your retirement money is at a managed pension fund or if you are affiliated with a college endowment, you'll want to be sure your investments align with your values. Talk to your money manager about which specific ESG criteria they're using.

Further, if you're like the women I surveyed, you'll be pleased to note that each of the issues you care about can be addressed through ESG investing. As we saw with the example in the previous chapter, climate change is high on the list of risk-management priorities across the industry meaning that the financial industry is poised to assist investors in collectively acting on this global issue. But if gun control is high on your list of priorities, you can also integrate companies with strong ESG ratings in this area in ways that continue to meet your preferred risk vs. return criteria.

And if you're concerned about the wage gap between men and women, you can join other like-minded investors to file shareholder resolutions to start a dialogue around this issue. Remember, the most important benefit of ESG investing is that it takes your singular voice and amplifies it. The power of ESG lies in taking collective action.

Let's take a break here. You now have enough information to know whether you're interested in ESG investing. And you know all that you need to know about ESG if you plan to invest your assets using a financial advisor. As mentioned previously, the numbers of advisors utilizing ESG portfolios are relatively low. So, do your homework and find someone who is authentically committed to the cause. The next chapter includes an overview of how best to find a suitable advisor.

If you're interested in constructing your own ESG portfolio, or you just want more investment education, keep reading as the next three chapters provide the more practical knowledge required to help you get started.

CHAPTER 4

Using Stocks to Incorporate ESG into Your Portfolio

If you're reading this book, then you've probably been recycling for years now. Maybe you buy your produce at the farmers' market and make an effort to support local businesses, especially around the holidays. You may even have expressed outrage on social media in the wake of the Marjory Stoneman Douglas mass shooting. Whatever the case, you're engaged and interested in doing your part to make the world a better place.

Yet, you may wonder if your actions are effective or if there's more you could be doing. I'm not suggesting you "live off the grid" or spend even more of your free time volunteering. In fact, I find there is often a misconception about changing the world, especially among boomer women. It goes something like this: if you want to make a difference, you've got to sacrifice your own happiness. Let's shatter that illusion now. By using ESG principles, you can actually make more of an impact while continuing to meet your financial goals. And the best part is you don't have to rearrange your life to do it. I'm happy to bring you the news that when it comes to values-based investing, women (finally) *can* have it all.

In this chapter, I'll discuss the practical steps you can take to incorporate ESG factors into your stock portfolio. But before diving in, let's see if it's worth going through the trouble by reviewing a real-life example of how individual shareholders changed the behavior of two of the largest public companies traded on the U.S stock exchange.

ESG Success Story: Collective Action Makes a Difference

I often hear skeptics who reject the notion that large corporations want or will make meaningful changes in policy in response to shareholder demands. You, too, may be skeptical about how much actual change ESG can bring about. You would be amazed, however, to learn what companies can do if they either have the will or are nudged by shareholders into finding the will to promote social change.

The Challenge

This success story featuring Monster Beverage Co. (parent company of Monster Energy drinks) shows that rapid change is not only possible, it's also good for business and for shareholders. The story begins back in 2016 when KnowTheChain, a partnership of ESG watch dogs, gave Monster a zero rating—yes, ZERO—because of concerns about slave labor practices in its sugar supply chain.

After an unproductive conversation where management insisted their supply chain was at low risk for unethical labor practices, even though the sugar industry is well known around the world for forced labor issues, *As You Sow*, a shareholder advocacy non-profit, was authorized to file a shareholder resolution on behalf of an individual investor with Monster's board. The resolution received the backing of 20% of Monster's shareholders—yes, shareholders are people like you and me. Monster's leadership got the message.

The Results

Two months later—MONTHS, not years—Monster hired a third party to perform a supply chain audit. It turns out that Monster was in fact buying sugar from countries with slave labor red flag warnings. Over the next three months, Monster:

1. Created a web page devoted to the issue of slavery in the sugar industry
2. Completed a survey of 80 percent of its suppliers
3. Trained internal staff to recognize red flags
4. Began building a training platform for suppliers

And the best part is Monster has committed to meeting particular milestones designed to reduce forced labor practices in the sugar supply line going forward.[71] As You Sow checked in with Monster at the end of 2019 and Monster had already beaten their 2021 milestones.

Additionally, As You Sow followed a similar process with General Mills to step up strategies for reducing pesticide use in its agricultural supply chain. In 2018, 31% of shareholders supported a proposal asking General Mills to adopt regenerative farming practices and to reduce pesticide use. This strong message from shareholders brought about change. The company has outlined specific ways they will measure progress on their pesticide reduction goals and issued new requirements for farmers supplying raw materials.[72]

These examples of shareholder success stories show how values-based investing can make a difference and how quickly companies can push through changes when they are incentivized to act. Could you imagine achieving the same results through the political system or the nonprofit sector? At the very least, these methods would take much longer to bring about such quantifiable positive results.

There's another lesson to highlight here as well. The Monster Beverage Company success story, in particular, shows how retail investors (that's individual shareholders like you and me) can gain the leverage that has, until recently, only been available to institutional investors who manage large pension funds and endowments. Monster provides a perfect illustration of how shareholders can use ESG tools to make a real difference.

Shareholder Advocacy Gives YOU—the Individual Investor—Power

As an individual shareholder, you have the right to vote on issues that could affect your investments. The problem is that as an individual investor, your vote can easily be drowned out by large institutional investors, such as large pension funds and endowments, with larger ownership interests. The solution is for individual investors to mobilize, pool their resources, and vote as a block.

This organizational capacity is the value of partnering with shareholder advocacy groups like *As You Sow*. Founded in 1992, *As You Sow*, run by CEO Andrew Behar, is now the nation's number one not-for-profit leader in shareholder advocacy. On Andrew's watch, *As You Sow* is developing a sustainability scorecard for each company listed in the S&P 500. Take a look at their mission statement:

> *"As You Sow promotes environmental and social corporate responsibility through shareholder advocacy, coalition building and innovative legal strategies. Our efforts create large-scale systemic change by establishing sustainable and equitable corporate practices."*

As You Sow provides sustainability information on individual companies as well as mutual funds and Exchange Traded Funds (ETFs). So if you are holding an ETF (think of it like a "basket of stocks") with hundreds of securities, for instance, you can run it through each of *As You Sow*'s six fund "tools" to see where your fund stands in terms of the following categories: Fossil Fuels, Gender Equality, Guns, Weapons, Deforestation, and Tobacco.[73] But what if you discover one of your mutual funds doesn't perform well enough, according to your standards, along ESG lines? Should you divest the fund? Perhaps, but first consider all your options. Where shareholder advocacy groups like *As You Sow* aim to make a real difference is in organizing and mobilizing shareholders like you and me. Together, our voices are amplified.

Are you surprised to learn that when you own a mutual fund or ETF, you have an ownership stake in all the companies within that "basket of stocks?" It's true! So why not start thinking like an owner? Let me remind you, your wealth gives you power and influence. Together shareholders can steer the future of companies around the world. So even if what I'm about to suggest feels counterintuitive, consciously choosing to hold onto shares of companies whose policies do *not* align with your values for the purpose of influencing their behavior may be exactly the right thing to do. This strategy, referred to as "hold and influence," is one that *As You Sow* along with niche fund managers are actively pursuing.

Andrew reports that women investors in audiences to whom he speaks all around the country are demanding their capital be used to create a safe, just, and sustainable world. "It gives me hope that there is a hunger for how we do this," he says. *As You Sow* is a great test case for how investors with ESG values can bring about change by banding together and urging companies to make positive changes. And by the way, Andrew and his team are not going to companies like Monster and General Mills and demanding changes that could put them out of business. The best part is that shareholder advocacy actually improves value by removing risks that may negatively impact shareholder value. So, the companies benefit too.

As You Sow is shifting the paradigm when it comes to ESG investing. "Companies really need to adopt, as part of their DNA, a stakeholder view of capitalism. If they don't adapt, they will be in trouble," says Behar. "Companies like ExxonMobil, which are determined to stick to the old paradigm, will eventually go out of business as more investors demand changes that their competitors are adopting." This is also, by the way, how ESG investing can be expected to potentially reduce risk for investors.

You can review some of the other changes that have been achieved through shareholder advocacy on *As You Sow*'s website. They have an impressive timeline showing all the changes that have come about through their work (e.g., June 1993: Revlon agrees to remove toxic chemicals from nail polish; February 2000: Hershey agrees not to use sugar from GMO beets[74]). You can also see current and past shareholder resolutions regarding climate change, diversity, and governance issues on their Resolutions Tracker as well.[75]

ESG Ratings and Your Stock Portfolio

If you have been in the investment game for a while, you likely already own stocks. Assuming you have your stock allocation determined, you then have the choice of selecting either individual stocks or holding a basket of stocks that have been bundled together, either in the form of exchange-traded funds (ETFs) or mutual funds. You can find ETFs and mutual funds in virtually every niche, with virtually every kind of trading style, with virtually every kind of ESG flavor. So this is an easy place to start when it comes to adjusting your investment portfolio to achieve your ESG goals.

Note that at my firm, we generally recommend exchange-traded funds (ETFs) and mutual funds rather than individual securities, given that *funds* are, by definition, a basket of stocks and therefore, diversified. This reduces what is referred to as "single stock risk," the risk that any one stock will significantly decline in value due to an idiosyncratic impairment. For example, new technologies, tax law changes, or even fraud can cause a single company to decline in value, as we saw in the case of Volkswagen.

Another reason to use ETFs and mutual funds to achieve your ESG goals is that the largest of these funds will generally have a huge share of the investor market, making it desirable for any public company to be included in the fund line-up. This gives investors in these funds an additional bargaining chip. When you work with a fund manager who is committed to honoring shareholder values, companies tend to pay attention rather than risk being excluded from the fund.

Iyassu Essayas, director of ESG research at Parnassus, where the largest ESG fund in the U.S. (the Parnassus Fund with over $27B in assets) is managed, explains how this works. He emphasizes that Parnassus seeks to build a collaborative relationship with companies included in their funds.[76] By regularly consulting with these companies and establishing open lines of communication, Parnassus provides valuable feedback on what matters most to their investors, while also encouraging action toward better sustainability.

From the companies' perspective, the risk of being thrown out of a fund with, for example, a 5% market share is something to be taken very seriously. Contrast this with being an individual shareholder with a few shares of a large corporation. Your lone voice carries little to no weight. This is the advantage of choosing funds with ESG criteria in mind: almost by definition, other investors who think like you will be seeking out these funds, thereby pooling their investment dollars with yours and consequently amplifying your voice.

How Do You Make Stock Selections?

If utilizing an advisor, you won't need to do that much choosing on your own. You will discuss your ESG goals with your advisor, perhaps fill out a questionnaire with your preferences, and your advisor will determine an investment strategy that best balances your ESG preferences with your risk/return profile.

Alternatively, you may want to build a portfolio on your own. Whether utilizing individual stocks, ETFs, or mutual funds, you'll want to know how each ranks in terms of sustainability. While this can be a daunting task for any individual investor, the ratings system provides a good starting point. As mentioned previously, there are over one hundred ESG rating agencies. The names of these ratings agencies are likely familiar to you because these are often the same agencies that are involved in credit ratings and other ways to evaluate public and private companies. Top among these are Morningstar, Bloomberg ESG Data Service, Corporate Knights Global 100, Dow Jones Sustainability Index (DJSI), Institutional Shareholder Services (ISS), MSCI ESG Research, RepRisk, and Thomson Reuters ESG Research Data.

Each of these agencies provides ESG ratings for hundreds of public companies. You (or your advisor) can use ratings from these agencies to build out the stock portion of your portfolio.

Sound simple? Yes. And no.

ESG criteria for investing are relatively new with reporting standards woefully lagging the rhetoric. Ratings agencies continue to discuss and debate the best ways to define ESG ratings— making the ratings system a work in progress. As we might expect, the lack of standardization and regulation has resulted in various ratings agencies using varying methodologies, potentially deriving different ratings for the very same company. So, it's important to do more digging.

Further, companies themselves are often guilty of jumping on the ESG bandwagon as a way to curry investor favor, rather than as a way to actually create positive social change. Sadly, much of the ESG criteria being evaluated by ratings agencies is often self-reported creating obvious conflicts of interest. The practice of misleading investors with respect to ESG practices is known as "greenwashing"—a play on the term "whitewashing," which is used to describe the practice of hiding or "painting over" the truth in order to cast oneself in a better light. Examples of this practice include labeling a product as recyclable when, in fact, only the exterior packaging is biodegradable and not the contents; or spinning statistics by claiming that green standards have been improved by 50% when the overall focus on green standards has gone from 2% to 3%. Such practices are clearly misleading and reveal a lack of commitment to ESG policies.

Despite these shortcomings, *ESG ratings can not only be informative, but they can potentially reduce your risk.* Consider, for example, how MSCI (one of the top ratings agencies) flagged the following corporate scandals:

Equifax

In August 2016, MSCI downgraded Equifax to a CCC (the lowest possible rating) a full year before Equifax confirmed the cybersecurity breach that put millions of Americans at risk of credit fraud.

Wells Fargo

In November 2015, MSCI downgraded Wells Fargo to a B, again, almost one year before Wells Fargo was faced with a $185M fine due to allegations Wells Fargo was opening accounts and charging fees without customer permission. In November of 2016, Wells Fargo was downgraded again to a CCC (the lowest possible rating), nine months before Wells Fargo was sued for wrongly charging customers for auto insurance.

Valeant Pharmaceuticals

In May 2015, Valeant was downgraded to a CCC rating, six months before fraud allegations were asserted with respect to Valeant and its drug pricing practices.

Volkswagen

Between 2013 and 2015, MSCI began to flag elevated warranty claims and deteriorating corporate governance practices. In March 2015, Volkswagen admitted that it installed emissions cheating software in 11 million vehicles.

Had more consumers been aware of these ratings, millions of investment dollars could have been saved. More importantly, inquiries into company policies may have resulted in problems being brought to light earlier.[77] So, while imperfect, there is enough evidence to suggest that good ESG ratings can not only influence corporate behavior but can also be an effective method of reducing risk within your portfolio. Meanwhile, ESG ratings continue to improve, as the industry takes note of the lack of reporting standards.

In 2011, the Sustainability Accounting Standards Board (SASB) was created to standardize the *material* ESG criteria being reported across numerous industries. SASB identifies material criteria as any information that would affect the judgment of an informed investor. The point is to protect investors from falling prey to laudable corporate claims that are nothing more than greenwashing. In November of 2018, the SASB codified the first set of ESG standards covering 77 different industries, making significant progress toward standardization.

Additionally, shining a spotlight on ESG issues is almost certainly the best way to improve the reliability of ESG rankings. There is increasing evidence that this light is coming in and will continue to shine: the rise of ESG in recent years has been enormous, with an estimated $20 trillion invested in this space around the world. As mentioned previously, this represents a full 26% of all profession-ally managed assets, albeit in the institutional space.[78] Investor awareness followed by investor pressure will almost assuredly re-sult in more standardization surrounding ESG reporting going for-ward. Given this evolution, I see this book as being on the forefront of a movement that is just starting to grow.

How to Incorporate ESG Criteria Into Your Portfolio

The most important thing to keep in mind is this: if you are interested in a specific cause, you can't simply pick one company or one fund that supports that cause. You *must* build and maintain a diversified portfolio with numerous asset classes, even while you choose funds with high ESG ratings. This is the only way to achieve index-like returns, reduce risk, and work toward long term financial security.

At my firm, we have developed fully diversified portfolios—across all asset classes—that incorporate ESG criteria. Our core portfolios are made up primarily of stock and bond funds (for more on incorporating ESG in the bond space, read the next chapter), both domestic and international, with the addition of several non-traditional investments in real estate, infrastructure, farmland and timber.

For our higher net worth clients, we also have alternative invest-ments available such as middle market lending funds, private real estate funds, and private equity. I discuss these alternative invest-ments in Chapter 6. For now, let's focus on how best to incorporate ESG into a more traditional portfolio.

Step 1: Find an Advisor Who Understands Your Unique Needs

If you prefer to build your own portfolio, you can skip this section. However, if you prefer to use an advisor, you will want to find someone:

1. With whom you can establish a good connection
2. With ESG knowledge
3. Who is a *fiduciary*

CONNECTION

Women and men look for different traits in a financial advisor. So, if you have been using your husband's advisor and your husband passes away, you may want to find a new advisor with whom you feel more connected. This is not at all uncommon as studies show that 70% of widows leave their financial professional within one year of being widowed.[79]

Additionally, studies have shown that when employing a professional, we women generally prefer a more holistic relationship—seeking to be understood in more ways than just our pocketbooks.[80] Therefore, finding an advisor who understands our values and life goals—someone who really "gets" us—is the most critical part of the equation. This is especially true if you're interested in values-based investing since your values are as much a part of your investment strategy as is your risk tolerance.

It's no surprise that men and women look for different traits in a financial advisor because men and women are different kinds of investors. Studies show that women have a long view when it comes to investing, focusing more on security than returns. We are generally less likely to follow a hot stock tip, get angry and dump a stock on a whim or trade frequently. Fortunately, because of our naturally steady investment temperament, we earn, on average, investment returns that are 1.2% or more higher per year than our male counterparts.[81]

While these trends are generally true, when it comes to *values-based* investing, women behave differently. In fact, a recent study shows that when it comes to values-based investing, women are "more often prepared to be the risk-takers and trailblazers," with a whopping 84% saying they are interested in sustainable investing.[82]

Despite evidence of women's prowess when it comes to investing, women are often ridiculed—either talked down to or dismissed entirely by advisors who expect buy-in of investment strategies that may not "feel" right. And while many of today's financial firms claim to "hear" women's unique perspectives, they continually offer the same investment strategies for women as their male clients, essentially doing nothing more than changing the font to pink in their marketing materials.

Don't be fooled by this gimmick. It is vital to find an advisor who understands your goals and your values in addition to your investment style. Look for an authentic relationship, one that is respectful of your more prudent, dual-mandate investment style.

ESG KNOWLEDGE

It has only been in recent years that individual retail investors—that is, people like you and me—have gained the knowledge and the access required to successfully invest with an ESG mandate. As a result, there aren't many financial advisors or even firms catering to high net worth individuals who offer real ESG investing, particularly across multiple asset classes. It may be easy enough to buy one ESG fund, but is the fund actually engaging with corporations to make a difference? And what about the rest of your portfolio, such as bonds, real estate, private equity, and other forms of alternative investments? You'll want to do careful research to find an advisor who truly understands the ESG landscape and is not simply "greenwashing" their own firm.

Don't be afraid to start a conversation with your advisor about ESG. Many individual investors do not take advantage of the ESG options available to them simply because they and their advisors are unaware of such options. Or, in some cases, advisors know about ESG options, but don't believe ESG investments are smart investments and will, therefore, not recommend them to clients.

One study conducted by *InvestmentNews Research* found notable differences in attitudes toward ESG-factor investing by male and female advisors. Recall that 53% of advisors constructing portfolios using ESG criteria are female, and of the female advisors who aren't doing so, nearly all said they would at least consider it. By contrast, male advisors are three times more likely than female advisors to dig in their heels against ESG—26% of male advisors say they are not using ESG criteria and will not consider doing so.[83] So whether you, as an individual investor, have the opportunity to invest using an ESG mandate could depend on whether you have a male or female advisor.

FIDUCIARY

Finally, it is imperative to find an advisor at a firm that is mutually aligned with your investment success. Unfortunately, not all firms are created equal in this respect, and sadly, the financial services industry has very effectively blurred the distinctions between the different pricing models. The financial model of the firm you are contemplating should be a key factor in your decision-making process.

As an investor, your number one goal is to find someone who can offer you objective advice with the least amount of personal gain when advising you. For this reason, I recommend you look for a fiduciary financial advisor. A fiduciary is legally and ethically required to act in your best interest. This means, for instance, your financial advisor is legally and ethically bound not to recommend high-risk or high-fee investments that may not be suitable for you. If you do not work with a fiduciary, you are at risk of taking costly advice from advisors who may be padding their own pockets rather than looking out for your financial interests.

Whether you choose to build your own portfolio, or decide to utilize a financial advisor, it is important to educate yourself on the basic terms and concepts of the investing world. If utilizing an advisor, you don't need to become an expert—your advisor is there to provide expert advice—but you will want to know enough to understand *how* your money is being invested and *why*. Most importantly, you'll want to know enough to confidently describe your natural investment temperament, your risk tolerance, and the values-based investment platform you seek.

There are many ways to educate yourself. For example, you can embark on your own self-education by reading personal finance books and articles, taking a course, or even joining an investment club. You should also feel comfortable relying on your financial advisor to help educate you. Be wary of any advisor who doesn't want to spend the time to help you understand their process. An informed investor is a smart investor.

Once you have educated yourself, decided to build your own portfolio or chosen an advisor with whom you connect, who understands the ESG and values-based investing landscape, and who is committed to investing your money according to what's in your own best interest, it's time to figure out your ESG strategy.

Step 2: Determine Your Preferred Level of Engagement

When I first introduced how ESG works in Chapter 2, I distinguished between two approaches to ESG offered by Parametric: passive ownership and active ownership. With the former, you can specify how much of your stock portfolio you wish to allocate to ESG-friendly funds. But with this indirect approach, you will likely not be actively participating with other shareholders in voting proxies or filing shareholder resolutions. With active ownership, however, you will join other shareholders to file resolutions and vote by proxy on proposed changes to company policy. This is a more direct approach to engagement.

Contrast this with some of the biggest fund managers such as BlackRock and Vanguard who are more indirectly engaged with companies on behalf of shareholders. While these managers say they embrace sustainable investing and ESG principles, when it comes to shareholder advocacy, they often don't engage at all. BlackRock only supported 23% of climate-related shareholder proposals in the 2017-2018 proxy voting season, for example.[84] So, if your portfolio is being invested through one of the bigger fund managers, you may not be getting much bang for your buck, so to speak.

With that said, these large ESG index funds do send a strong *indirect* message to companies. They may not heavily engage with company management or participate strongly in proxy voting and shareholder resolutions, but they certainly do favor one company over another when it comes to their fund lineup. For example, the more sustainable companies typically have a higher weighting in the fund than the least sustainable companies. Given the market cap of these behemoth funds and the strong desire of companies to be included in such funds, it stands to reason that over time, companies may modify their sustainability behavior in order to increase their access to the fund.

What About Your Retirement Plans?

When considering how your retirement money is working for you, keep in mind also that 74% of all ESG-factor investing is at the institutional level, driven primarily by pension funds, endowments, and private foundations.[85] While this point was made previously, it's important to note that if your state or federal pension fund is being managed by an institutional money manager, your assets may not be supporting the causes you most care about.

According to a report released by the U.S. Sustainable Investment Forum (US SIF), asset managers at institutional firms identify "climate change" as the most important ESG issue in asset-weighted terms with more than $3 trillion being invested in climate-related funds, followed by tobacco-related restrictions at $2.89 trillion, and "conflict risk" (i.e., terrorist or repressive regimes) coming in at $2.26 trillion.[86]

These are important issues, for sure, but when I asked the women taking my Women, Wealth, and ESG survey (wealthy, boomer women from across the U.S. and across the political spectrum) to rank the importance of social issues relevant to ESG investing, they ranked ethics/moral/religious/family decline (41%) and lack of gun control (25%) above climate change. In fact, only 23% ranked climate change as the most important issue we face. Tobacco product restrictions and conflict risk both ranked near the bottom of the list. So, if you're invested at an institutional level through a pension fund, for example, your investments may not align with the ESG issues you actually care about.

Top 3 ESG issues according to financial institutions (in asset-weighted terms):

1. Climate change
2. Tobacco-related restrictions
3. Conflict-risk (i.e., terrorism and repressive regimes)

Top 3 ESG issues according to wealthy boomer women (2019 Women, Wealth, and ESG Study):

1. Ethics/moral/religious/family decline
2. Lack of gun control
3. Environment/pollution/climate change

Finally, if you have a 401(k) plan at work, you probably don't have a sustainable investing option since, unfortunately, 96% of 401(k)s don't offer an ESG option.[87] In the final chapter, I'll discuss strategies you can use to talk to your benefits department about ESG and how your employer can make the switch.

Step 3: Choose a Platform that Allows for More Customization

Whether you prefer a more direct or indirect ESG approach, the one challenge when utilizing ETFs and mutual funds remains that, ultimately, you are relying on someone else to select a basket of stocks and causes you are supporting. If you prefer greater control over the contents of your portfolio, while maintaining high levels of diversification, you can utilize a fund manager or investment vehicle that provides a custom option.

At my firm, we allocate a portion of our equity holdings to Parametric for this very purpose. Through Parametric, our clients can screen industries they want to avoid completely (note this is more of a Socially Responsible Investing (SRI) strategy) or choose a portfolio with an ESG tilt (does not exclude entire industries but chooses best in class from every sector) from a customizable menu of options. In this way, our clients may choose to hold the securities of companies whose values do *not* align with their own for the purpose of exerting pressure and influencing corporate behavior.

You may now be wondering whether a "hold and influence" strategy is better than divesting the stock of companies whose policies don't align with your values. In the gun example we reviewed earlier, recall Dick's Sporting Goods and Walmart changed their gun sales strategies following public outcry and the threat of economic risk. But was it the divestment of their stocks by their shareholders or the negative publicity gone viral that triggered their reaction? Perhaps it was the fear of declining retail sales that prompted the quick response.

Now, don't get me wrong. I'm not saying that divestment can't work in the right situations (for example, South Africa). I'm only saying that creating change does not *always* come from divesting company stocks. For some social issues, like female representation on public boards, we have found different strategies to be more effective. The case study below demonstrates how the hold and influence strategy works in these situations.

Hold and Influence Case Study: Increasing the Number of Women on Public Boards

You may (or may not) be surprised to learn that the U.S. lags behind *all* other developed countries on gender representation in the boardroom.[88] As of September 2019, according to Equilar, Inc., a governance data firm, women held only 20% of all public board seats at U.S. companies.[89] This reality not only flies in the face of equal opportunity, but generates real concern about the potentially harmful impact of homogeneous thinking on company performance. Suppose you care deeply about this issue and you want to use your wealth to influence change here. How would you make this happen?

First, take a look at your securities. Suppose you discover you hold stock in a company with no female representation at its board level. What do you do? Assuming you do not own a majority stake, selling your shares, while perhaps constituting a show of personal rebellion, will likely not get more women board members instituted. Remember that, by definition, when you sell your shares, someone else is buying them. So there's really no direct impact felt by the company unless a *huge* block of investors suddenly wants to sell which would bring down the stock price. But unless investors communicate their reasoning, even this loss of value won't make much of an impact since huge blocks of shares are traded every day simply to rebalance portfolios. Perhaps there is a better strategy you could employ.

As an investor, in some cases, you can rely on a fund manager like Parametric to actively engage with companies one-on-one while keeping your values and financial interests at heart. At Parametric, the dominant strategy in cases like gender representation is to hold shares in companies whose policies are not sustainable while attempting to influence their behavior through proxy voting and shareholder resolutions. Does this work?

Case in point: Parametric recently used their "hold and influence" strategy with respect to the issue of women on corporate boards and pay disparity by voting on shareholder resolutions related to these matters. These resolutions asked management to improve the state of gender parity on their boards by finding qualified women and minority candidates to nominate.

The Result: Initially 33 board resolutions were filed by a range of asset owners. 25 were withdrawn after receiving a positive response from the company, meaning no shareholder vote was even needed to influence companies to change their policies. Of the remaining eight, four went to vote and received double-digit support from shareholders including Parametric. At the same time, 31 resolutions were filed at U.S. companies related to gender and minority income disparity. Again, 23 were successfully withdrawn after positive company responses and four more received double-digit support.[90]

I had the opportunity to interview Jennifer Sireklove who leads the Investment Strategy Team at Parametric which is responsible for all aspects of Parametric's equity-based investment strategies. Here's what she had to say about the major differences between the biggest asset management funds, e.g., BlackRock and Vanguard, and smaller fund managers like Parametric who are taking the lead on establishing effective ESG approaches:

"In all cases, divesting is a very, very indirect tool to effecting corporate change."

Trading for the purposes of divestment in and of itself doesn't impact the company's asset value or provide any communication to management since company stocks are traded every day for all sorts of reasons. Take for example, the issue of fossil fuels. "Unlike apartheid, which is often held up as a divestment success story, the world can't [yet] live without fossil fuels." Instead, we need to encourage companies to use and produce fossil fuels more wisely while we invest in the technologies to replace them. Divestment alone won't achieve that. However, when investors combine active ownership with screening methods, they can make a huge difference—and this is what Parametric enables shareholders to do most efficiently.

Highlights from My Interview with Jennifer Sireklove

Q. How does Parametric approach ESG? How does the process work? What is unique about your approach?

A. In 2015, Parametric decided to make ESG strategies a major focus on their investment platform. The goal of the platform is to make ESG-factor investing as simple for individual investors as all other types of mutual funds, ETFs, or bond funds. To make this possible, we combine custom screening with Parametric-led active ownership. For individual investors, this means that the opportunity to align your values with other like-minded individuals is amplified through this platform.

We aren't afraid to vote against management if appropriate. We are committed to the dual mandate of aligning with shareholders' values and preserving their net worth. Because Parametric is so client-centric, we get a lot of feedback about what our clients care about and want to prioritize. This helps us decide what to focus on. For example, the partnership between Parametric and As You Sow arose because of a client's request.

Here's how the partnership works: As You Sow notifies Parametric of any shareholder resolutions they are planning to file during the next round of proxy voting. Because As You Sow is not an asset manager or asset owner, they rely on other investors to file the resolution. Parametric notifies interested clients of these opportunities to co-file which helps As You Sow get the resolution on the ballot so it can be voted on.

This is true whether our individual investor has chosen to customize a portfolio or simply go into an existing fund that aligns with their values.

Q. What are the most important things investors interested in ESG issues should know? How should they go about educating themselves so they can be most effective?

A. This depends on your goals as an investor. Is your objective to own companies that align with your values? Then, you need to know your own values and simply buy a fund that fits. There are public resources available to help with this, like As You Sow, and you can also look to your advisor for recommendations. But make sure to find a fund that also aligns with your personal risk tolerance and diversification goals.

*If, however, your goal is to make a greater impact by changing corporate behavior, then you may want to be more involved in understanding how your shares are being voted. Some people wonder why companies would listen if an investor **won't** sell her shares, but the answer is simple: shareholders have the power to vote out members sitting on the board of the companies they own. So, it's in the board members' best interest to pay attention to their shareholders. Companies do actively solicit feedback from shareholders and can be quite receptive to good ideas. This is why it can be more effective to own and influence than divest and why investing in a shareholder-centric fund can amplify your individual voice.*

Q. Where do you see the future of ESG heading? What's on the horizon for Parametric and ESG?

A. There is growing awareness that ESG investing can be about improving overall market returns, not just beating the market. For example, the government pension fund of Japan is actually paying fund managers for active ownership, also called stewardship. Their logic is that because they are such a large investor and own the entire market, they benefit more by making "beta," or market returns, more sustainable rather than hunting for "alpha," or market relative returns, via ESG. This is a real game changer. It shows how these larger funds are starting to think about the future and the long-term value of taking ESG factors into account. Companies as a whole are looking at themselves as partners in sustainability. Investing does not have to be a zero-sum game, and as investors recognize this, companies are starting to take notice.

The lessons in this chapter are clear: Collectively, women can pool their investment resources and use their leverage as shareholders to bring about social change. We see evidence of this in success stories like Monster Beverage Co. and General Mills. We see evidence of it with the issue of gender representation in the boardroom too. Different issues and industries require different strategies.

So, it makes sense to educate yourself. You can either do it alone or you can find an advisor who knows you, knows ESG, and knows how to balance your financial needs with your values. Incorporating ESG into your stock portfolio can be a complicated process, but not impossible. The right financial team can help. Let's next see how to apply ESG to bonds.

How to incorporate ESG into your stock portfolio:

Step 1: Determine if you will build your own portfolio or use an advisor. If using an advisor, find someone with whom you can establish a good *connection,* someone with *ESG knowledge,* and someone who is a *fiduciary.*

Step 2: Determine what level of engagement you prefer and choose fund managers accordingly.

Step 3: If you want to be more involved with selecting the companies making up your portfolio and/or you want to become a shareholder activist, find a platform that allows for more customization.

CHAPTER 5

Using Bonds to Incorporate ESG into Your Portfolio

Up to this point, I've been focusing on ESG issues in relation to stocks, but your diversified portfolio should also include bonds. And while there's no question that, to date, the rise of ESG-related investing has been focused primarily on public stocks, it appears a massive shift is in progress as more and more investors understand that bonds and ESG make natural bedfellows. So, let's talk bonds.

You may recall that while a stock represents an ownership stake in a company, a bond is a loan to a company or government entity. Bonds can be issued by private or public corporations but can also include loans you make to the U.S. Federal Government, states or municipalities, government-related agencies (e.g., Fannie Mae or Freddie Mac), or foreign governments. In exchange for the loan, you (the investor) receive interest payments during the bond's term — and ultimately, you receive your original investment (the loan amount) back on the bond's maturity date.

Given the media attention directed toward stocks (ESG-related or otherwise), you may find it surprising to learn that the world's total bond market is greater than the world's total stock market ($100 trillion in bonds[91] vs. $78 trillion in stocks[92]). And in the U.S., the total amount of debt outstanding in 2017 was $40.7 trillion, including more than $14.4 trillion in United States Treasury debt, more than $9.2 trillion in mortgage-related bonds, more than $8.8 trillion in corporate bonds, and more than $3.8 trillion in municipal bonds.[93] This means the ESG potential impact could be even greater in the bond space than in equities. Some experts even predict that fixed income (i.e., bonds) could become the core of sustainable investing in the near future.[94]

ESG Success Story: Renewable Energy as an ESG Municipal Bond Opportunity

Experts in the bond market often focus on ESG risks, rather than opportunities. According to Gurtin Municipal Bond Management[95], this makes sense given that the downside of potential credit losses due environment, social, and governance issues usually looms larger than the upside of potential gains. There is, however, at least one area that represents a clear ESG bond opportunity for cities, counties, school districts, and other municipal bond issuers — it is renewable energy. There is a growing movement to power 100% of a community's electricity needs with renewable or carbon-neutral energy. As of this publication, 145 cities, 12 counties, and eight states have committed to going down this path[96].

How does the move to 100% renewable energy benefit investors? As Gurtin notes, cities and counties that position themselves as leaders in renewable energy will be prepared to meet higher standards and future environmental regulations coming down from state or federal governments. Rather than having to take on huge debts to meet stringent regulations later, these communities will be able to make improvements at a pace that they choose. This will also likely create more dialogue within these communities about other sustainability issues, such as zero carbon emissions in transportation and climate change adaptation strategies. All of this can provide a boost to a community's creditworthiness, making their debt issue not only sustainable but financially savvy.

Another opportunity includes the reputational boost gained from being viewed as a sustainable and forward-looking place to live. These communities will be more attractive to younger generations graduating and looking for a place to start their careers and families. This reputational boost can also help communities draw more like-minded businesses and tourists. For example, the community of Georgetown, Texas estimates that the move to sourcing 100% renewable energy netted it more than 2.1 billion online impressions.[97]

While there are other ESG opportunities in the bond space, environmental concerns are at the forefront of bond issuers minds for many reasons. Consequently, "green" bonds have become one of the most popular areas for investors. 2019 saw a record number of so-called "green" bonds being issued too (i.e., bonds issued by governments, public or private corporations, municipal entities, and other bond-issuing institutions for the purposes of delivering environmental as well as financial returns). Over $200 billion green bonds were issued in 2019, funding everything from improved corporate environmental practices to public transportation projects. The market for green bonds has exploded: In 2015, it was less than $50 billion and a decade ago, it was under $5 billion.[98]

ESG is on the Rise in the Bond Space

ESG is on the rise in the bond space for multiple reasons, not the least of which is the recognition that an organization's practices surrounding Environmental, Social, and Governance issues can have a material impact on its long-term creditworthiness. Secondly, as in the stock or equity space, there are simply more options in the bond space for investors to choose from now than ever before. For instance, according to the Forum for Sustainable and Responsible Investing (US SIF), at least 17 corporate bond funds with a focus on environmental, sustainable, and governance factors are currently available in the market.[99] In fact, debt financing is now the principal source of financing for most public companies. In addition, municipal bond issuance reached a global high in 2018 of $167 billion, representing a 15-fold increase since 2013.[100]

And finally, the UN Sustainable Development Goals (adopted by all 193 U.N. members) with a target date of 2030 means that the long-term horizon for social and environmental projects is well suited for fixed-income bonds which investors tend to hold longer than stocks. Meeting the goals within this initiative will require $3-$5 trillion per year, the majority of which will need to come from the private sector in the form of bonds. This represents one of the most successful uses of ESG criteria to impact the area of climate change and its impact on the world economy. According to the Harvard Law School Forum on Corporate Governance and Financial Regulation, 40% of the world's 250 largest corporations have started referring to the SDGs in their annual reports.[101]

To understand the sustainability strategy of bond funds, investors may want to read the fund's prospectus, annual reports, and manager commentary. Be aware of what you're getting: some funds are simply composed of ESG-leading corporate bonds that track indexes, while others take a more active approach. As in the stock space, this approach allows the fund to work with bond issuers that may be screened out on the grounds of ESG factors alone, promoting more sustainable behavior. Ultimately, you can seek out impact reports to see what kind of measurable results these funds are producing in terms of their ESG impact.[102]

By integrating ESG into your bond portfolio, your dollars can impact social change both domestically and across the globe, influencing everything from the Hudson Yards development in NYC, which is the largest real estate development in the U.S. by area, to gender equality in China. While I don't have the space here for a deep dive into all the different facets of the ESG bond market, below you'll find an overview of the various types of bonds you can access.

Corporate Bonds

As the name implies, corporate bonds are utilized by public companies wishing to raise capital. Often when companies need to raise funds, they issue bonds rather than borrowing from banks because the terms are more favorable and the interest rates are lower in the bond market. Because corporate bonds are issued by the same public companies issuing stocks (e.g., Apple issued a $1.5 billion green bond initiative in 2018 to fund the company's conversion to renewable energy and an increase in its use of biodegradable materials[103]), the same ESG ratings provided by the ratings agencies can be used by values-based investors for the company's bond issuances. And as in the case of stocks, your voice will carry far more weight if pooled with other investors in an ESG bond fund that engages with companies to promote sustainable behavior. As mentioned previously, the credit ratings agencies are also moving toward ESG ratings.

Mortgage-Backed Bonds

A mortgage-backed bond, as the name implies, is a bond backed by a mortgage or a pool of mortgages. This type of bond is typically more secure because in the event of a default, the bond issuer can sell the underlying real estate related to the bond to pay back the debt. (For a lesson in what happens when loans default and the bond issuer is unable to sell off the real estate at a price sufficient to pay off the loan, refer to the Subprime Mortgage Crisis—a major cause of the 2008 Financial Crisis).

Note that when homeowners pay their mortgages, a portion of their interest payments are used to fund dividends to the mortgage bond investors. So as long as most of the homeowners in the pool make their mortgage payments, a mortgage-backed bond offers a secure and reliable return. History has taught us that these loans must be carefully underwritten and that the terms of the loan carefully scrutinized.

In June 2019, Freddie Mac issued its first green bond designed to provide financing for homeowners who make their homes more environmentally friendly (e.g., making energy or water efficiency upgrades) within a 2-year timeframe. The program also targets affordable rental units for workers who serve their communities (for example, teachers, nurses, and firefighters). Per the government agency itself, this move was designed to meet the rising demand from investors seeking fixed income options in the ESG space.[104]

Treasury Bonds

Government-backed bonds are another type of bond that is a natural fit with ESG investing. As an investor living in the U.S., you're probably most familiar with U.S. Federal Government bonds issued by the Treasury Department. Treasury bonds have varying terms with maturities ranging from 10 to 30 years and are considered "risk-free" investments as they are backed by the full faith and credit of the United States Treasury.

The $41 trillion U.S. government bond market is the largest in the world and makes up the majority of the funds invested in the total bond market in the U.S.[105] Obviously, the federal government has a huge role to play in enacting policies that will drive social change.

Sovereign Debt

In addition to loaning money to the U.S. Federal Government, investors in the bond market can loan money to the governments of foreign nations. When considering ESG investing relative to an entire country, the implications are far wider than when investing in the debt of a single company. For example, when purchasing the government bonds of Venezuela, Goldman Sachs was condemned for propping up a corrupt and oppressive government.[106] Others would argue that not loaning money to Venezuela serves only to further injure an already oppressed population.

Given the range of activities governments perform, it's unrealistic to expect any government will be beyond reproach from the strictest ESG perspective. Can we honestly say, for example, that in its many activities, the U.S. government always has sustainable behavior? Whether you choose to invest in countries with strong ESG ratings, despite questionable practices in other areas, is up to you and your own sense of personal values.

Municipal Bonds

Municipal bonds are primarily used to fund state and local government projects. Many municipal bonds already focus on Environmental, Social, and Governance issues making them a natural fit for ESG-conscious investors. As an example, muni bonds are used to fund infrastructure projects related to public hospitals, education, airports, mass transit, and others. Additionally, cities use municipal bonds often, though not always, to fund environmentally sound projects including efficient, renewable energy; clean water; sustainable waste management and eco-friendly transportation.

Many ESG investors also find municipal bonds to be a great fit because they often fund projects that contribute to the social good such as low-income housing, public university infrastructure, and other not-for-profit projects. Not only does the money contribute to the social good, these projects are also governed by rules and regulations designed to support equality, fairness, and diversity.[107]

Besides the ESG benefits of municipal bonds, there are tax benefits (whereas the interest payments you receive from corporate bonds are taxable, the interest you receive from municipal bonds will never be subject to federal taxes. And if you buy bonds in your home state, you won't pay state or local taxes either). Note also that historically, municipal bonds are 50 to 100 times less likely to default than corporate bonds.[108] With over 50,000 state governments, local governments, and other entities issuing municipal bonds (vs. 10,000 corporate bond issuers), it's not hard to see why the muni market is so popular among values-based investors.[109]

I sat down with Emily Robare, Head of ESG Research at Gurtin Municipal Bond Management and she shared Gurtin's perspective on how investors can strive to make a difference through their municipal bond investments.

Interview with Emily Robare, Head of ESG Research at Gurtin Municipal Bond Management

Q. Do you agree that municipal bonds are a natural fit for ESG factors and why or why not?

A. The great benefit of investing in the municipal bond market has always been that when you take into account the low risk of default plus the emphasis on investing in local communities, then yes, these bonds can be a natural fit for socially responsible investing. Since you're investing in cities, counties, and states— you're helping to grow and reinvent those communities directly. But we can take this a step further when it comes to ESG issues. For example, in the area of climate change, municipal bond investors can engage with local governments and encourage them to be forward-thinking in adapting to and mitigating their climate risks.

Unlike the corporate market, there are no organizations like As You Sow bringing together municipal bond investors to engage with issuers. So at Gurtin, we have been working to find innovative ways to engage with municipalities on ESG issues. Given the size and breadth of the municipal market, we've worked with larger organizations that represent local governments in order to reach a larger number of municipal bond issuers all at once, as well as partnering with nonprofits, like CDP (formerly the Carbon Disclosure Project). Our goal is twofold: to increase issuer disclosure of ESG risks, such as climate risk, as well as communicate to local governments that these types of risks are important to investors. This not only can potentially reduce the risk of nonpayment of debt but can also potentially help U.S. state and local governments move faster to address climate change and other significant ESG concerns.

Q. What do most investors not understand well when it comes to investing in municipal bonds?

A. Most don't understand that while it's true that municipal bonds are a natural fit for ESG, there's more to it than that. We don't want investors to assume that because it's a muni, it's ESG. There are cities issuing debt for projects that are not sustainable, as well. Just as with stock funds, bond fund investors need to do their homework. Gurtin has a specially curated social advancement strategy for investors who want to focus on socially responsible factors, especially community sustainability.

Q. What is unique about your approach to ESG and municipal bonds?

A. Gurtin's engagement practices with municipalities are on the forefront of the municipal bond space. Many cities and communities don't think about their exposure to climate change. They may not have thought about how they can reduce emissions and the impact they can collectively have. Bonds significantly outnumber stocks when it comes to the number of issuers —there are 50,000 municipal issuers in the country, which is way more than the companies in the S&P 500.

Q. How should investors assess the quality of ESG ratings from the ratings agencies or their bond managers?

A. This is a good question because there is no comprehensive ESG ratings agency for municipal bonds, which means investors and bond managers need to do more independent research on ESG factors for municipal bonds. We are seeing certain credit rating agencies such as Moody's, S&P, and Fitch, putting out more information and data on ESG risks, but that information is not as robust as it could be. Investors can ask their bond managers what types of ESG risk factors are being incorporated into credit analysis, as well as the type of engagement that managers are undertaking with issuers. It's important for investors to think about not just the potential impact of their investments, but also the ESG risks they might be exposed to. For example, the potential for a big cultural shift around climate change is here and if things shift quickly in how the market views climate risk, investors could lose money if holding onto bonds that have significant exposure to climate risks.

CHAPTER 6

Using Alternative Investments to Incorporate ESG into Your Portfolio

Once you've incorporated ESG factors into your core holdings (stocks and bonds), you may want to consider an allocation to alternative investments — that is, investments that are not traditional stocks and bonds. The potential advantage to holding alternative investments is that they are typically less correlated to the public markets, thereby providing another level of diversification. And as we know, more diversification generally means reduced risk for the overall portfolio.

Many investors are finding it increasingly difficult to generate income from their portfolios given the extremely low interest rate environment in which we find ourselves. Long gone are the days of clipping bond coupons with a reasonable income stream. Some alternative investments, especially in the case of real estate, can often offer higher income in addition to higher return potential in a tax efficient way.

Equally important, however, is the potential impact of ESG investing utilizing alternative investments. These private funds are often more targeted in their efforts, making them suitable for those investors who wish to see direct results. Remember, however, that there is "no free lunch" (as my mom used to say). These investments come with their own sets of risks, often higher when viewed in isolation. Also, they are typically illiquid for a period of time, most often 5-10 years, so you'll want to consider your cash needs. However, when incorporated into a well-diversified portfolio, I believe alternative investments can lower overall risk while enhancing both income and returns.

Below I describe some examples to help you better understand how each alternative investment has its own flavor of ESG. If customization is attractive to you when it comes to making investment decisions, alternative investment funds can be an especially good option. But, again, I only recommend this strategy in combination with a traditional, well-diversified portfolio suitable to your risk tolerance and cash needs.

Private Real Estate Success Story: Doing Good for Communities While Doing Well for Investors

When I think of real estate development, I typically think about environmental disruption. I think of trees being leveled and land being developed with one motivation only—maximizing dollars per acre. Developers (especially those who come into a community from outside) are met often with great disdain, if not protest, from the local community.

What if I told you, however, that there are developers out there who are actually sought after by communities that lure them with tax rebates and incentives as a way to gain their expertise in helping them improve their communities? Enter Grubb Properties, a real estate investment firm headquartered in Charlotte, NC.

When I first met Clay Grubb, I was immediately taken with his holistic approach to real estate development. Clay wasn't just focused on the financial aspects of a real estate project, but more on how it would enhance the overall community and how it would fit in with changing demographic trends.

To me, his strategy seemed brilliant. He explained that his focus was to develop "live, work, play" communities in urban locations. This sounded simple enough, but the marketing strategy for making these retail and apartment complexes a success included the goal of attracting millennial women. I wondered about the reasoning behind this. Clay put it this way: "Wherever the girls go, the boys will follow," proving, yet again, when values align with investment decisions, everyone wins.

The Grubb projects often incorporate their trademarked Link Apartments®. These sleek, contemporary living spaces come with large walk-in closets, full-size appliances, and big bathrooms. There's very little wasted space in these apartments, which are smaller than the typical apartment (though you'd never know from the inside because they are so cleverly designed) and, therefore, also a bit less expensive.

Grubb is a "green" builder, earning LEED or other similar green certifications for their sustainable building practices (full disclosure: I am personally an investor in Grubb Properties). Investors in Grubb funds enjoy the benefits of rental income that is tax deferred while also promoting good building and environmental practices. There is no clear cutting of forests and residents are not chaining themselves to bulldozers trying to thwart the developer.

How attractive.

The goal of creating live, work, and play communities that require few to no cars for residents makes a lot of sense given the ratio of cars to people in the United States—a whopping seven parking spaces per person, according to Grubb. This strategy, when executed in congested urban areas with-old fashioned, sprawling buildings connected by large, wasteful parking lots, can make a real difference.

By rezoning the parking spaces, creating more living, working, and retail spaces, and encouraging people who want to live and work in the same location to move in, everyone wins. Surface runoff water is reduced; the need for cars is reduced; and the community is revitalized with young people who are flocking to cities for work.

You may be wondering how this strategy works without creating a parking shortage. The parking that remains is shared. Some residents need parking at night, and employees need parking during the day, creating a nice synergy for shared parking. Also, residents of these live, work, play communities want more public transit. As the demand for public transportation rises, it stands to reason that cities will begin to fund transit projects in greater numbers to accommodate these sustainable living areas. There are good reasons to believe if these live, work, and play communities catch on in American cities, we will see fewer cars on the roads.

With all these benefits, it's no wonder that Grubb is being lured with tax credits and rebates from local municipalities in North Carolina and surrounding states. So, how do investors take advantage of this opportunity? It's important to ask for it—but be sure to do your due diligence, either independently or in conjunction with your financial advisor. Note that this type of sustainable real estate has become increasingly available to savvy investors in recent years, but it wasn't until 2017 that an even newer concept became available—one that includes greater tax benefits while explicitly honoring ESG concerns—the Qualified Opportunity Zone Fund (QOF).

Qualified Opportunity Zone Funds

Always at the forefront, Grubb Properties recently launched its own QOF—a concept introduced by the new Tax Cuts and Jobs Act of 2017. Designed to boost economically struggling communities, this legislation provides powerful tax incentives to investors, while also promoting investment in depressed communities.

Here's how it works: Let's say you have a large capital gain, for example, from the sale of a stock or a real estate holding. Normally you would have to pay capital gains tax on your profit (the difference between what you paid and what you sold the investment for). The federal tax rate for realized capital gains is currently a maximum 20%. In addition, depending on where you live, you would likely owe state taxes on the gain. However, if you instead take your capital gain and reinvest it in an Opportunity Zone Fund within 180 days after the sale, you can defer paying taxes on the gain for up to seven years, depending on the year in which the gain was incurred. This allows you to reinvest pre-tax dollars (more money than post-tax dollars). But beyond the deferment benefit, you get a discount on the tax due when it is ultimately paid. In this way, you've not only deferred the tax due, but you actually pay less. And this is just the beginning.

Let's say you double the money you place in the QOF. Assuming you hold this investment for a total of ten years, you *never* have to pay taxes on this second gain. The tax benefits resulting from this legislation have become so sought after that numerous firms are attempting to develop Opportunity Zone Funds.

Remember, though, that the fund is only as good as its ability to generate positive returns, both financially and economically for its residents. I've seen many fly-by-night operations come and go, luring investors with their ESG mandate and the promise of tax benefits, while failing economically. Therefore, it is essential to review these opportunities with a critical eye and utilize only a real estate firm with a proven track record.

As with any other investment, there is always risk. An Opportunity Zone Fund may increase or decrease in value over the holding period. Also, just as there are unique benefits, there are unique risks involved. QOF is a newer option and the IRS and the Treasury Department are still working out the specifics of how this legislation will work in the long term. So, it does not make sense to pursue an QOF simply for the tax benefit. The underlying investments must make good economic sense in and of themselves excluding any tax benefits if you're to succeed financially.

Grubb Properties is one of a handful of Opportunity Zone Funds we have found in which we have confidence. Relatively small, locally sourced, Grubb is a niche player with a deep knowledge of the communities they serve. Their track record and numbers are impressive. Since 2002, the company has completed more than $1 billion in real estate investment transactions. Per Clay, the sum total of all transactions generated a compounded net weighted-average return in excess of 40%.

Interview with Clay Grubb on His Unique Real Estate Business Model

Q. Can you explain your approach to real estate development?

A. We have become laser-focused on trying to provide more affordable living opportunities in urban markets. 80% of Americans cannot afford the average price of a new home in America; 40% cannot afford the average price of an apartment; and 20 million Americans pay more than 50% of their gross income in rent. These numbers show that affordable housing is quickly becoming a major crisis in urban cities throughout the U.S. We're playing a small part in making this less of an issue.

This is where the demand is (i.e., affordable housing). Traditionally, it hasn't been as profitable to play in this niche, even though the high end in real estate is over supplied. But we're maintaining our margins by leveraging relationships with municipalities that want affordable housing in urban areas. The apartments we build are $400 per month less than the luxury apartments or roughly 15% below market rates in the areas where we build. We feel this is right in line with ESG principles. In fact, we're going through an ESG assessment with GRESB within the next eight months. We also have a Director of Sustainability. So we are really going all in here.

Q. Can you talk about a recent success story?

A. Montford Park in Charlotte is one of our recent successes. Before we invested, Montford Park was a fairly rundown neighborhood (although it had been a thriving community back in the 1960s). The Park Road Shopping Center had recently been sold to a larger firm that planned to invest heavily in its revitalization. We felt the timing was right and purchased two office buildings just two blocks away.

The office buildings were half occupied. We came in and worked with the 650 residents to help brand the community. Together, we created a neighborhood association. We renovated the office buildings and built our Link Apartment® product. The two office buildings are now 90% occupied. The first stage of apartments will open in 2020 and we're getting started on the second phase now.

We've really done a lot to create a sense of community at Montford Park. In addition to making it more resident-friendly, four of the restaurants in the neighborhood have been named to the top 50 list in Charlotte! It's a vibrant live, work, play community. Not only that, but in relation to ESG factors, this is the most sustainable project in Charlotte. The utility bills are fractions of what they were before we developed the community. We put in new windows to prevent overheating, improved internal air quality, abated the asbestos, and made it overall more environmentally clean.

We're also working to connect the community to the greenway for biking to downtown. As a result of these improvements, a tax base of $15M has now become $250M. So, not only are these communities good for individuals who are flocking here, and investors who are enjoying the tax incentives, they're good for the municipalities where we're building.

Q. What motivated you to launch an Opportunity Zone Fund? What gives you confidence that this fund will be successful?

A. Four of our last ten projects were already in "opportunity zones" before the 2017 tax legislation ever passed. This is an area that we've always worked in, therefore, it fits naturally within the context of an OZF. Regardless of the tax incentives, creating more affordable housing has been a part of our business model for years. We're pleased that the legislation is starting to catch up.

Q: Developers are often criticized for pushing out low income people. What do you do to mitigate the risks of gentrification?

A: We dedicate a full 10% of the OZF inflows toward mitigating the impact of gentrification. If you reduce setbacks and eliminate side yards, communities can end up with the equivalent of two smaller affordable houses, rather than one high-end house. At Grubb Properties, all of our properties have a self-imposed rental cap for residents who've lived with us for five years or longer, encouraging younger residents and those with lower incomes to stay in the city rather than fleeing to the suburbs. This plan is very different from government-imposed rent control where landlords often end up unhappy.

As a result, government-imposed arrangements artificially limit interest in developing these types of communities. However, when landlords themselves impose the caps on rent, it demonstrates that they actually care about their tenants, shattering the stereotypical concept of a "slumlord." This, in turn, creates both a tremendous desire to live in the community and take pride in it, with renters taking care of their property as if it's their own home. For example, long term residents will alert Grubb to any problems, rather than looking the other way.

Q. What's on the horizon for Grubb Properties?

A. We are proud of what we're doing to revitalize the communities where we're invested. This kind of property development is in high demand in virtually every community in the country. Our goal is to grow and build on our successes. We have no interest in changing the model. We'll likely get more selective about the locations we choose and are starting to see opportunities in this niche for purchasing properties at lower prices. As we look to the future, we think the next ten years will be really good, but we worry about the following ten years.

With boomers aging and the strain this will put on Medicare and the health system, we worry about a downturn in the market and how that might affect our investment base. As a result, we're looking to universities, hospitals, and medical systems to partner with us. We'll look for new investment opportunities near state and federal government offices as well.

All of these strategies will hold up well during any potential economic downturn. We also believe our sustainable business model aligns with future transportation needs. On average, 15% of an American's income is spent on cars. But cars are a depreciating asset. So a recession will lower consumer demand for cars and more Americans will be looking for areas with mass transit and the ability to walk or ride to work.

Private Equity

Qualified investors also often incorporate private equity investments into their portfolios. As the name implies, private equity is an investment in a private company that does not have access to public markets or traditional bank financing. These investments are riskier than traditional asset classes (e.g., stocks and bonds) and, therefore, most appropriate for institutional investors, university endowments, or wealthy individuals. With that said, generally, with a higher risk, comes a higher reward.

Among the riskiest forms of private equity is an area known as venture capital—i.e., a private investment made in a startup company with long-term growth potential. Venture capital started as a niche activity at the end of World War II but has evolved into a sophisticated industry that propels entrepreneurship and innovation. Ownership in both private equity and venture capital is often achieved through a limited partnership structure with the primary difference being that venture capital companies are generally seeking funds for the first time, while private equity financing is reserved for bigger, more established companies.

Within the venture capital space, there are many opportunities for values-based investors. If you care about social issues, you can invest in companies doing great things to impact very specific areas where you want to make a difference. But, again, if one of your goals is to make an impact while reducing your risk and seeing a financial return on your investment, then your best opportunities will be ones where you can pool your assets with other like-minded investors. One such VC fund, Sustain VC, backs innovative entrepreneurs that share a vision of a sustainable, more equitable, and healthier world.

Justin Desrosiers (Durham, NC) and founder, Sky Lance (Boston, MA), Managing Principals at SustainVC, explained how they invest for-profit dollars into early stage companies that are making a positive difference in the world.

Interview with Justin Desrosiers and Sky Lance
Managing Principals at SustainVC

Q. How did you get into this space?

A. Sky Lance: I was an early investor in the tech space in the 1980s in both Boston and Silicon Valley. Having been successful there, I then expanded into private equity, venture funds, and buyout funds. Later, in 1990, I co-founded a private equity firm known today as Windjammer Capital Investors. The target for Windjammer was to build very large funds ($500M) incorporating established businesses. But I quickly realized the more successful my partners and I became - and the more we moved into financing larger and larger companies - the more no one would even notice if we went out of business given the numerous alternative financing options available to these companies.

Counterintuitive as it sounds, purchasing large widget companies made me feel irrelevant. I wanted to make a bigger impact, so when a friend introduced me to the concept of impact investing—not philanthropy, but a form of investing that accomplishes the same goals using for-profit models—I jumped on the idea. In 2007, I founded SustainVC and now, together with other investors, we fund early-stage, high-impact companies with the goal of helping them reach their financial and impact goals.

One of our goals is to fund predominantly women-led and minority-led businesses. Currently, 56% of the businesses we fund fit this demographic profile. The businesses we support, in turn, employ more women and minorities.

Q. Can you talk about a recent success story? How have you impacted the work of early stage companies while also ensuring that investors see a strong return?

A. Justin Desrosiers: We decided to fund a company founded by two women in the climate change arena. It was a new company and they were doing great things, but they were in the very early stages and hadn't yet turned a profit. Solstice Power Technologies was initially founded as a not-for-profit with the aim of getting solar energy into the hands of low-income Americans. Because most solar developers require customers to have a high FICO credit score (650-700+) and own their roofs, over half of Americans do not qualify for rooftop solar. Solstice came up with a new algorithm for figuring out the likelihood of someone paying their utility bill—removing the reliance on FICO scores.

Customer data suggest that this new EnergyScore represents a 40% improvement over FICO in predicting utility bill payment behaviors. So, their innovative model allows low- and middle-income customers to subscribe to solar farms and see savings on their electric bills. Solstice Power Technologies offers a service platform for solar developers that makes it easier for them to find low-income customers, do the billing, and benefit the environment. Additionally, they have a scalable business model and it is working. Solstice is available in 14 states, as well as Washington, D.C.

Another of our success stories is Boston Heart Diagnostics. This company was led by a female CEO and provided a huge return for investors while helping to save lives and improve quality of life. BHD came up with a special blood test that measures subfractions of cholesterol, and when combined with other blood tests, is paving the way for more personalized medicine. The targeted heart tests allow patients to see results they weren't seeing with prior testing. What started with a few hundred thousand in annual revenues ultimately sold with revenues of $97M per year.

Q. How do you decide which early-stage companies are smart investments in terms of generating both social and financial returns?

A. Because early-stage private companies do not have the track records or regulatory checks and balances we see with public markets, we know we need to do our homework to protect our investors. "We screen companies with a lens toward impact and simultaneously look at the business model," says Lance. We look carefully at the management team as well to determine whether they can be agile when running the business when things get difficult. We ask, 'do they have a solution to address the issues in the market?' Altogether our team puts in over 200 hours of due diligence for each new investment.

SustainVC's business model definitely fits with the dual mandate philosophy. Their investors are not taking a haircut on venture returns just because they fund social impact projects. The Internal Rate of Return (IRR) ranges from single digits to over 100% so it's fair to say there's a broad range of potential returns.

To give you some perspective here, anything in the 30-40% range is a good IRR over a five-year period, for instance, in the venture capital industry. The early-stage venture capital game is a high risk, high reward game. So far, for realized transactions (i.e., early-stage companies with positive returns), they've seen returns of over 30%. But they also carry several unrealized companies (i.e., early-stage companies that have not yet become profitable) in the portfolio.

Yes, there have also been losses. To date, SustainVC has invested in 32 companies, eight of which have been losses. They've also seen seven exits where companies have been successfully sold. Based on the remaining portfolio company performance to date, over two-thirds of the investments will likely be successful, putting SustainVC into a class of high-level in-

vestment opportunities. Lance and Desrosiers understand that positive re-turns lead to a positive impact when it comes to startups with ESG values. So, they aim to invest in sustainable companies with growth potential.

Q. Where do you see impact investing or ESG factor investing heading in the future? What's on the horizon for SustainVC?

A. Lance: If you're a startup business looking to raise $500k to $5M, you're in "no man's land." Maybe you've tapped your friends and family already, but you're not quite ready for Series A funding (an average of $13.4M). This is our niche. SustainVC wants to stay in this market segment because this is where we feel we can make the biggest difference.

SustainVC is seeing more and more interest from women investors who care about the world around them. 40% of our investors in the first fund were women, and, so far, 33% of investors in the new fund are women. More investors are starting to acknowledge that women and minority business owners are underserved and more investors want to do what they can to lift up these businesses, which provides a great business opportunity for SustainVC.

At my firm, private alternative investments currently make up as much as 25% of an individual portfolio. Keep in mind that these vehicles are typically available only to those individuals that are Accredited Investors (individuals with investable assets of $1M) or Qualified Purchasers (individuals with investable assets greater than $5M).

The alternative investments we utilize at my firm currently include private real estate funds, middle market lending funds, private equity, and venture capital, though the types of alternative investments we offer are subject to change given market conditions and availability. Our clients with an ESG mandate, therefore, can participate in a line-up of private funds that have ESG policies in place to supplement their public stock and bond holdings.

Given where we are in the market cycle—on the heels of a ten-year bull market—it probably makes sense to incorporate at least some of these investments into your portfolio, assuming you meet the required net worth criteria. Alternative investments are by far the most flexible way to incorporate ESG criteria into your portfolio. These types of private investments allow you to choose to put your money into specific ESG-friendly companies and industries such as alternative energy.

Because non-publicly traded alternative investments are by definition, *private*, there is no public reporting required. This means that while investors can rely on reporting frameworks provided by the Sustainability Accounting Standards Board (SASB) for their holdings in public companies, the same information is often not tracked or disclosed by private companies. This creates a group of potential investments with even "looser" standards than those expected within the public markets. Unfortunately, there are currently no recognized ratings for the numerous types of alternative investment opportunities that are available.

Without the benefit of the ratings agencies and with no disclosure requirements, how can you identify and invest in such alternative investments in accordance with your values? It's not easy. These investments are often not available to an individual retail investor and can only be accessed through an institutional money manager or your financial advisor. This area, in particular, is one where a good financial advisor can be invaluable.

ESG-minded advisors can not only provide access to these funds but can also provide research related to the investment's financial prospects, its suitability for your portfolio, and its ESG practices. Note that the better private investments understand that sustainability can influence not only investor interest, but also economic performance, though again, "greenwashing" is something about which to remain mindful.

Be sure your advisory firm has a good investment team that can vet each of these investments, review financial statements and performance, and actually talk to the company's management team while considering ESG criteria. As noted above, with alternative investments like Opportunity Zone Funds, it's especially important for firms to get to know how these funds operate and determine whether they are worth the risk. Again, the number of advisors who are well versed in ESG and take this kind of time to get to know these alternative investments well is still relatively low, so it's very important to find a good fit—someone who is both knowledgeable and a fiduciary to help you.

CHAPTER 7

Be the Change You Want to See

I started this book by saying I wasn't the kind of kid who would start UNICEF, and yet, here I am trying to start a social movement. What has changed? Obviously, a lot has changed about me and the world in which we live. But the main difference is that I believe change is possible in a way I couldn't have dreamed possible as an adolescent.

I'm also no longer that small Iranian immigrant child struggling to assimilate. I'm a woman on top of my profession. A female financial advisor finding success in a male-dominated industry. A woman whose clients seek out because they want more from their advisor and their investments. Most importantly, I am a woman who is passionate about the world in which we live and the social issues we face.

If you share my passion and are fed up with the lack of progress being made, here's my challenge to you: Why not try something new? Why not *be* the change you want to see? Why not put the power of up to $22 trillion dollars of wealth to work in creating a more sustainable world—a world that is more environmentally friendly, has better gun control, is more culturally diverse, more gender neutral, and more just.

Investing in line with your values is no longer a fad—it's here to stay. More importantly, it works. If you don't believe me, consider the following:

- As mentioned before, Dick's Sporting Goods and Walmart almost immediately changed their gun sales policies due purely to public outrage on social media coupled with economic risk as shareholders began to divest their stocks and threatened to boycott their stores.

- Monster Beverage Co. changed their sugar supply chain within months of being confronted by shareholders to better protect against modern day slavery.

- Since 2008, the World Bank has raised $13B by issuing more than 150 "green" bonds in 20 currencies for investors around the world.[110]

- Following the green bond model, over $500B has been issued in bonds promoting social issues and specific development projects in accordance with an ESG mandate—all since 2008.[111]

- Private investments such as Grubb Properties have helped revitalize dozens of communities while reducing carbon footprints, reducing wasted space, and building with green standards.

These examples are not even close to exhaustive in showcasing all the ways **public sentiment, *if channeled economically, can impact corporate behavior*.** But examples like these give me hope that meaningful, positive, and large-scale social change is possible. I also know this kind of change can't come about through the work of a single individual. It takes a collective effort. I hope you'll consider these words as your personal invitation to start putting your money where your values are.

If you're wondering how to get started, take a look at the following practical steps you can take immediately:

Do Something Now to Make a Difference!

1. Find the right Environmental, Social, and Governance (ESG) resources.

First, I can't emphasize enough the value of educating yourself, either on your own or through an advisor who really understands your financial needs, your appreciation for values-based investing, and how to balance both. Investing with an ESG mandate remains (for the time being) a specialized area requiring expertise. Given the current limitations of ESG ratings, remain wary. And if using an advisor, look for one who is experienced in this area, is happy to answer your questions, and has the resources to find answers to questions she doesn't know off the top of her head.

Second, look for fund managers, like Parametric, that not only offer a diverse ESG portfolio, but a strategy of direct "engagement." Remember that a "hold and influence" approach maintains diversification within your portfolio while also giving you and other like-minded investors the opportunity to put forth shareholder resolutions and use your proxy voting power to voice your values as a collective. There is no doubt that there is strength in numbers. Company leadership listens to shareholders who are organized and use their voting power to ask for reasonable policy changes.

Third, remember that your investment dollars can work for you in all asset classes, not just stocks. Consider bonds as well as alternative investments when making the switch to ESG.

While many financial advisors have taken note of the increased interest in ESG and sustainable investing criteria, few firms have taken *action* to make this a priority. Fortunately, I work with a team of professionals who are making sustainable investing a priority. Let's face it: most of us don't have the time and energy needed to research every company in the supply chain for each and every product we buy. This would be a daunting task. In fact, finding a solution to this problem is perhaps the most persuasive reason for investing with an ESG mandate.

When investors join forces, they can influence companies to operate in a way that is environmentally friendly, socially conscious, and governed in accordance with standards of transparency, diversity, and anti-corruption. In this way, we can all feel more confident that what we're buying supports our values. The more individual investors like you and I push for the kinds of changes I'm advocating throughout this book, the less the dual mandate philosophy of doing good while doing well financially will be considered a luxury or a niche market. It will become the norm. And at that point, real change will be within reach.

2. If you're still working, talk to your benefits department about ESG options.

ESG funds make up only a fraction of workplace retirement plans. As mentioned previously, in 2017, a mere 4% of defined contribution plans (401(k)s or 403(b)s) provided ESG options, according to a survey by the Plan Sponsor Council of America—and these ESG options represented less than 1% of total plan assets.[112] But as the demand for investments that contribute to the social good rises, employers will be motivated to add ESG options to their menu of retirement plan investments.

One actionable step you can take is to talk to your HR department about making ESG funds available for employees. Depending on the type of company you work for, this could be a tough sell, though. 401(k) sponsors tend to be conservative about making these types of changes, so be prepared for some pushback.

Also, most experts agree that ESG will only become more widely accessible in retirement plans when target date funds—funds that automatically reduce a participant's exposure to stocks as they approach retirement— begin to provide ESG options. One thing is for certain: employers will not add ESG options if they don't know employees want them. So, talk to your co-workers, get a group together, and talk to your benefits manager.

3. Form an investment group and read this book together!

To really move the needle on the issues that matter the most to women, we must talk to each other. I know that it might not be considered "ladylike" to talk about money with your particular social circle, but isn't it time to start changing this perception? Since when has the demand to be more "ladylike" ever benefited women as a whole? And it certainly doesn't benefit us in this case. Not talking about money leads us to believe, like the women in my survey, that women control only 36% of the wealth in the U.S. as opposed to the 51%-60% (and rising) we actually control. Not talking about money leads to the gender wage gap where women make only 79 cents on the dollar relative to men.[113] Not talking about money leads to the "power" gap that we face today.

So, one easy way to break down this barrier is to form an investment group where you talk about investing and support each other as you figure out your financial lives. Once you've formed your group, educate yourselves. Read books, including this one, and discuss how you can better advocate for yourselves and your values. If you'd like assistance from a professional, find an ESG-friendly and woman-friendly advisor (I know one who's quite savvy, with apologies for more shameless self-promotion). You can share information and brainstorm ways to put the power of your wealth into the social causes you care about the most.

4. Talk to your family, friends, neighbors, and colleagues about ESG. Spread the word!

I hope this book can be a conversation starter. I know that change can be painfully slow sometimes. I also know that investing with an ESG mandate is not a perfect system, but I'm encouraged by the research I have shared in these pages. We are making progress and the trends are pointing toward even more success over the next several years. With any luck, we are experiencing the cutting edge of a revolution in attitudes about investing with a dual mandate. I'm committed to doing what I can to spread the word. And I hope you will be inspired to do the same.

Final Thoughts

In the days and weeks following the school shooting at Marjory Stoneman Douglas, I remember feeling a shift. I remember watching ordinary Americans opening their eyes to new and different ways to make their voices heard. I remember—for the first time in a very long time—believing that social change is possible.

Change never happens overnight and because change, by definition, upsets the *status quo*, it will never be popular among those in positions of power. And this is precisely why it is up to us—women with more power than we realize—to raise our hands and call it out. I am more convinced now than ever before that bringing about the kind of change we want to see will require bypassing the traditional channels that have not only historically held women back, but have also left our world in environmental peril, allowed social injustice to thrive, and given corrupt governance the upper hand. We boomer women now have the power to do something about this. We can use our unprecedented wealth to make a difference, securing our financial futures while also securing a more sustainable world for future generations.

My aim in this book has been:

- To convince you that we women, who control 51-60% of the nation's wealth (up to $22 trillion and climbing), can harness our collective desire to make a positive impact in a world plagued by social injustice.

- To demonstrate that women operate in a "power" gap; we don't understand the power we have at our fingertips and are also timid about using it when we do.

- To show you that neither the ballot box nor your charitable activities alone can solve our social issues—we must leverage our wealth to influence the real power brokers of our society - public companies.

- To persuade you that ESG investing is the best vehicle through which to make this positive impact while also protecting your own financial well-being.

- To show you that regardless of party affiliation, we women care about the same social issues and are equally frustrated by our inability to bring about change using traditional means.

- To show you that NOW is the time to take action because NOW is the time we are on top.

I believe I have made my case. The only thing standing between you and what you want is inaction. Please, please—be the change you want to see.

About the Author

Haleh Moddasser is a Senior Financial Advisor at Stearns Financial Group and the Managing Partner of their Chapel Hill office. Over the last ten years, Haleh has built a practice devoted primarily to women and their financial empowerment, a topic about which she is passionate. In addition to her client engagements, Haleh has written extensively about women and finance and has been published widely in national media outlets such as Forbes, Barron's, Reuter's, Bloomberg, and Kiplinger's among others. Haleh has spoken at various national conferences including Schwab Impact and NAPFA's annual conference. Most recently, Haleh was a guest speaker at the Chan School of Public Health, Harvard.

In 2017, Haleh published her first book, *Gray Divorce, Silver Linings: A Woman's Guide to Divorce after Age 50* to address the financial implications of divorce among long time couples – a trend that is on the rise among aging boomers. Haleh's newest book, *Women On Top: Women, Wealth & Social* Change, is focused on ESG investing.

In the book, Haleh encourages women to invest their wealth with a mind toward doing good in the world while also doing well for themselves financially. By investing in sustainable companies, Haleh maintains that women can support social causes such as climate change, gender equality and more effective gun control while earning comparable returns. *Women on Top* will be available on Amazon in early 2020.

2019 Women, Wealth, and ESG Survey Summary

Methodology:

The rise of women's financial clout is one of the most important economic shifts we will see in our lifetimes. Not only are women generating and managing a significant amount of wealth, they are increasingly interested in finding new ways to put their wealth to work to support the causes they care about the most. It stands to reason that if women work together while controlling the majority of the nation's wealth, greater progress can be made.

Rather than guessing about the issues most women care about or reporting on purely anecdotal evidence based on my work with clients, I used an independent third-party research firm (Survey Monkey) to conduct a survey of approximately 500 women, from across the U.S. These women ranged in age from 55 to 75 and had USD $500k or more in investable assets, defined as including both retirement accounts and non-retirement accounts.[114]

Essentially, I surveyed wealthy boomer women living in the U.S. to find out how they perceive their ability to influence social change, what they know about ESG investing, and what social issues they most care about.

The results are enlightening. What follows are key insights about a growing and diverse group of women who are fundamentally rethinking the meaning of wealth and giving. Fortunately, women now, more than at any other time in history, are in a position to change the world their children will inherit.

Q1
Please select the option below that best applies to you:

Answered: 529   Skipped: 3,873

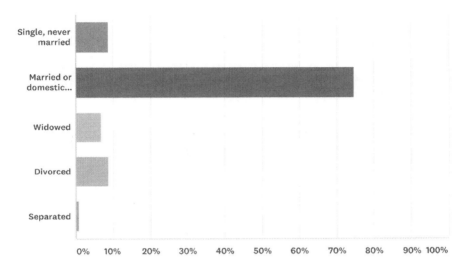

ANSWER CHOICES	RESPONSES	
Single, never married	8.70 %	46
Married or domestic partnership	74.67%	395
Widowed	6.99%	37
Divorced	8.88%	47
Separated	0.76%	4
TOTAL		529

Q2
The next question relates to the concept of ESG (Environmental, Social, Governance) or Sustainable Investing (SI).
Please select the option that best applies to you:

Answered: 534   Skipped: 3,868

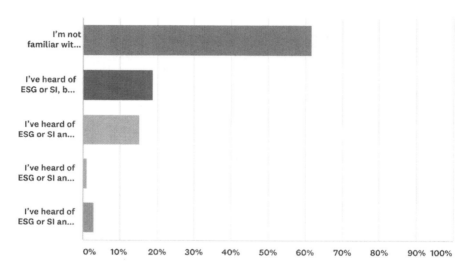

ANSWER CHOICES		RESPONSES
I'm not familiar with ESG or SI.	61.80 %	330
I've heard of ESG or SI, but I don't know much about it.	18.91%	101
I've heard of ESG or SI and am curious.	15.17%	81
I've heard of ESG or SI and am purposefully not investing using these criteria.	1.12%	6
I've heard of ESG or SI and am invested with an ESG mandate or using SI criteria now.	3.00%	16
TOTAL		534

Q3
Please indicate your level of agreement with the following statement: The U.S. political system has the ability to solve our social problems.

Answered: 528   Skipped: 3,874

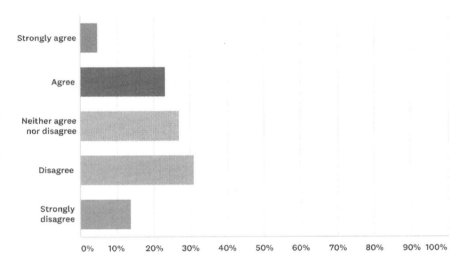

ANSWER CHOICES	RESPONSES	
Strongly agree	4.73 %	25
Agree	23.30%	123
Neither agree nor disagree	27.08%	143
Disagree	31.06%	164
Strongly disagree	13.83%	73
TOTAL		528

Q4
Please indicate your level of agreement with the following statement: Non-profit organizations and charities have the ability to solve our social problems.

Answered: 530   Skipped: 3,872

ANSWER CHOICES	RESPONSES	
Strongly agree	3.77%	20
Agree	28.87%	153
Neither agree nor disagree	36.79%	195
Disagree	23.96%	127
Strongly disagree	6.60%	35
TOTAL		530

Q5
Please indicate your level of agreement with the following statement: Public and private companies have the ability to bring about social change.

Answered: 531   Skipped: 3,871

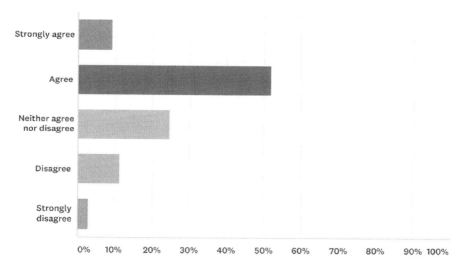

ANSWER CHOICES	RESPONSES	
Strongly agree	9.23%	49
Agree	51.79%	275
Neither agree nor disagree	24.67%	131
Disagree	11.30%	60
Strongly disagree	3.01%	16
TOTAL		**531**

Q6
As a percentage, how much of the nation's wealth would you estimate women control?

Answered: 529   Skipped: 3,873

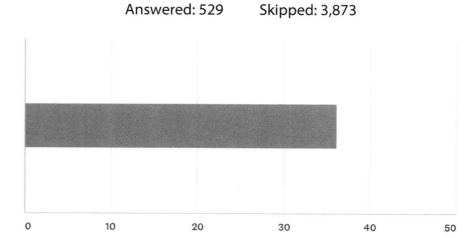

ANSWER CHOICES	AVERAGE NUMBER	TOTAL NUMBER	RESPONSES
	36	19,147	529
Total Respondents: 529			

Q7
Thinking about the past year, how much money have you donated to charity?

Answered: 533   Skipped: 3,869

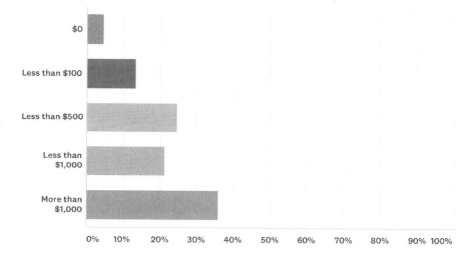

ANSWER CHOICES	RESPONSES	
$0	4.50%	24
Less than $100	13.32%	71
Less than $500	24.77%	132
Less than $1,000	21.39%	114
More than $1,000	36.02%	192
TOTAL		533

Q8
Please select the option that best applies to your political affiliation:

Answered: 533   Skipped: 3,869

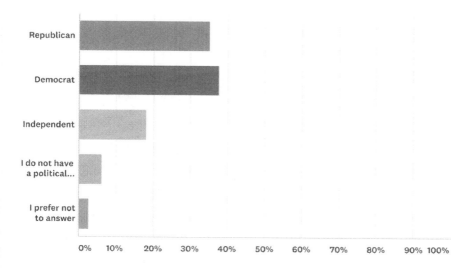

ANSWER CHOICES	RESPONSES	
Republican	35.08%	187
Democrat	37.71%	201
Independent	18.20%	97
I do not have a political affiliation	6.38%	34
I prefer not to answer	2.63%	14
TOTAL		533

Q9
Please indicate your level of agreement with the following, where prudent means "showing care or thought for the future:"

Answered: 526   Skipped: 3,876

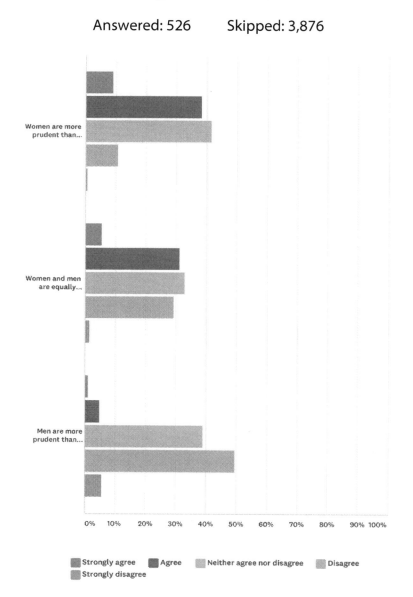

Women are more prudent than...

Women and men are equally...

Men are more prudent than...

0% 10% 20% 30% 40% 50% 60% 70% 80% 90% 100%

Strongly agree   Agree   Neither agree nor disagree   Disagree
Strongly disagree

	STRONGLY AGREE	AGREE	NEITHER AGREE NOR DISAGREE	DISAGREE	STRONGLY DISAGREE	TOTAL	WEIGHTED AVERAGE
Women are more prudent than men when it comes to money.	8.94% 47	38.21% 201	41.63% 219	10.65% 56	0.57% 3	526	2.56
Women and men are equally prudent when it comes to money.	5.34% 28	31.11% 163	32.82% 172	29.20% 8	1.53% 1	524	2.90
Men are more prudent than women when it comes to money.	1.15% 6	4.78% 25	39.01% 204	49.52% 259	5.54% 29	523	3.54

Q10
Please indicate your level of agreement with the following, where prudent means "showing care or thought for the future:"

Answered: 525   Skipped: 3,877

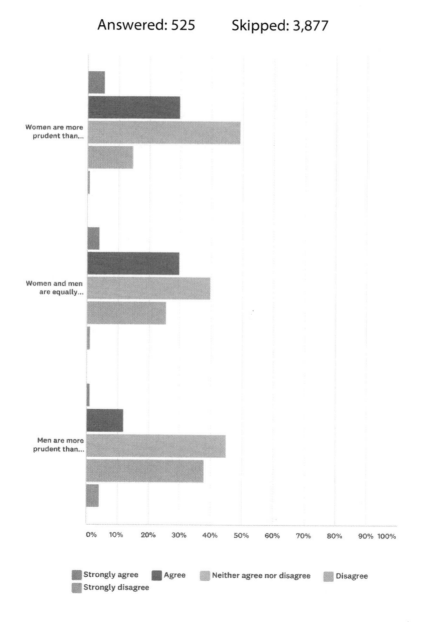

Strongly agree   Agree   Neither agree nor disagree   Disagree
Strongly disagree

	STRONGLY AGREE	AGREE	NEITHER AGREE NOR DISAGREE	DISAGREE	STRONGLY DISAGREE	TOTAL	WEIGHTED AVERAGE
Women are more prudent than men when it comes to investing.	5.53% 29	29.77% 156	49.24% 258	14.69% 77	0.76% 4	524	2.75
Women and men are equally prudent when it comes to investing.	4.02 % 21	29.64% 155	39.77% 208	25.43% 133	1.15% 6	523	2.90
Men are more prudent than women when it comes to investing.	0.95% 5	12.02% 63	45.04% 236	37.79% 198	4.20% 22	524	3.32

Q11
Please indicate your level of agreement
with the following, where risk averse means "cautious
or disinclined to take a chance:"

Answered: 526   Skipped: 3,876

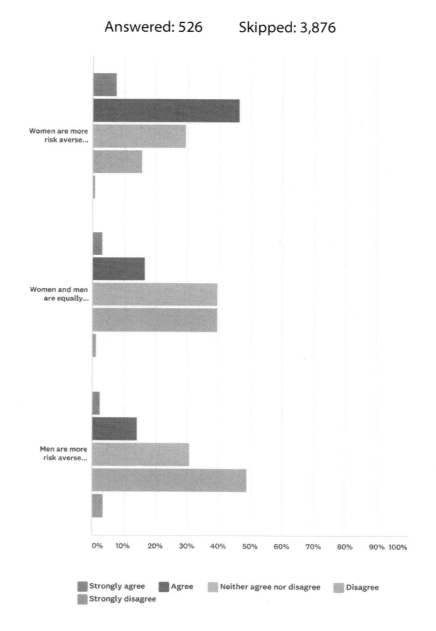

Strongly agree   Agree   Neither agree nor disagree   Disagree
Strongly disagree

	STRONGLY AGREE	AGREE	NEITHER AGREE NOR DISAGREE	DISAGREE	STRONGLY DISAGREE	TOTAL	WEIGHTED AVERAGE
Women are more risk averse than men when it comes to investing.	7.60% 40	46.39% 244	29.47% 155	15.78% 83	0.76% 4	526	2.56
Women and men are equally risk averse when it comes to investing.	3.06 % 16	16.44% 86	39.58% 207	39.58% 207	1.34% 7	523	3.20
Men are more risk averse than women when it comes to investing.	2.47% 13	14.26% 75	30.80% 162	48.86% 257	3.61% 19	526	3.37

Q12
Below is a list of issues our country faces today. Please choose the top 5 and rank them in terms of importance to you (1 = most important, 2 = second most important, etc.):

Answered: 499   Skipped: 3,903

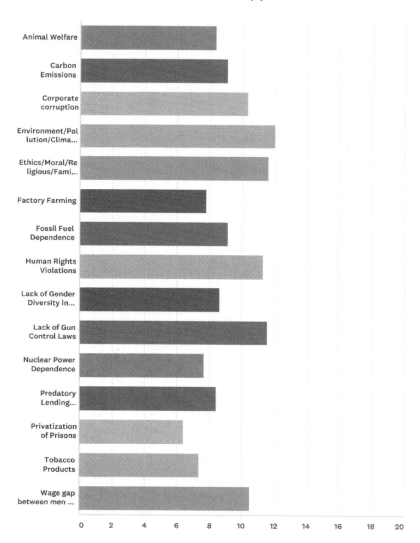

	1	2	3	4	5	6	7	8	9	10	11	12	13	14
Animal Welfare	1.88% 5	5.26% 14	10.53% 28	10.53% 28	14.66% 39	6.02% 16	6.02% 16	5.26% 14	4.14% 11	5.64% 15	6.39% 17	5.64% 15	5.64% 15	5.26% 14
Carbon Emissions	5.11% 14	9.12% 25	10.22% 28	11.68% 32	13.14% 36	5.47% 15	4.74% 13	4.38% 12	6.57% 18	5.11% 14	5.47% 15	5.84% 16	5.84% 16	3.65% 10
Corporate corruption	6.78% 23	14.45% 49	14.75% 50	12.68% 43	17.11% 58	3.54% 12	4.13% 14	4.42% 15	2.95% 10	4.13% 14	2.65% 9	4.42% 15	2.36% 8	2.06% 7
Environment/Pollution/Climate change	22.96% 91	23.23% 92	16.67% 66	9.34% 37	8.08% 32	1.52% 6	3.03% 12	2.27% 9	2.78% 11	1.26% 5	1.01% 4	2.02% 8	3.03% 12	1.52% 6
Ethics/Moral/Religious/Family decline	40.88% 148	10.77% 39	6.91% 25	6.08% 22	7.18% 26	3.59% 13	1.93% 7	2.76% 10	3.04% 11	3.04% 11	1.66% 6	3.04% 11	1.93% 7	3.04% 11
Factory Farming	1.69% 4	4.24% 10	5.93% 14	8.47% 20	10.59% 25	6.36% 15	6.36% 15	8.90% 21	6.78% 16	7.63% 18	8.90% 21	8.47% 20	7.20% 17	4.24% 10
Fossil Fuel Dependence	4.21% 12	7.72% 22	9.12% 26	15.06% 43	12.98% 37	7.02% 20	5.26% 15	5.26% 15	4.91% 14	4.56% 13	4.21% 12	6.32% 18	5.26% 15	5.26% 15
Human Rights Violations	12.64% 46	18.13% 66	17.31% 63	14.01% 51	13.46% 49	4.40% 16	2.20% 8	2.20% 8	3.02% 11	1.92% 7	3.02% 11	0.82% 3	2.20% 8	2.75% 10
Lack of Gender Diversity in Corporate Governance (e.g., too few female board members)	3.91% 10	7.81% 20	8.20% 21	10.55% 27	12.50% 32	6.59% 22	5.06% 13	6.25% 16	5.47% 14	3.91% 10	4.69% 12	4.69% 12	7.42% 19	5.86% 15
Lack of Gun Control Laws	25.41% 94	18.65% 69	13.24% 49	10.00% 37	7.57% 28	2.97% 11	2.70% 10	2.16% 8	1.62% 6	3.24% 12	2.16% 8	2.43% 9	2.16% 8	2.43% 9
Nuclear Power Dependence	3.43% 8	3.86% 9	5.15% 12	9.87% 23	9.87% 23	5.15% 12	7.30% 17	5.15% 12	7.30% 17	9.44% 22	6.44% 15	7.30% 17	6.01% 14	6.87% 16
Predatory Lending Practices	1.58% 4	7.11% 18	11.07% 28	11.07% 28	9.49% 24	5.53% 14	7.11% 18	6.72% 17	5.53% 14	5.14% 13	6.72% 17	5.93% 15	5.93% 15	6.32% 16
Privatization of Prisons	0.89% 2	3.11% 7	3.11% 7	5.78% 13	7.56% 17	4.44% 10	8.44% 19	5.78% 13	7.56% 17	5.33% 12	11.11% 25	6.67% 15	8.00% 18	12.00% 27
Tobacco Products	2.07% 5	3.72% 9	8.68% 21	9.50% 23	9.09% 22	3.31% 8	5.37% 13	5.37% 13	7.02% 17	7.85% 19	5.37% 13	7.85% 19	7.85% 19	9.09% 22
Wage gap between men and women	8.96% 30	13.43% 45	16.12% 54	18.81% 63	11.94% 40	1.79% 8	2.99% 10	3.88% 13	3.28% 11	3.28% 11	3.28% 11	1.79% 6	2.39% 8	3.88% 13

Q13
When making purchases, please select the option below that best applies. In this context, "values/ behaviors" would include, for example, a company policy to intentionally reduce carbon emissions:

Answered: 498   Skipped: 3,904

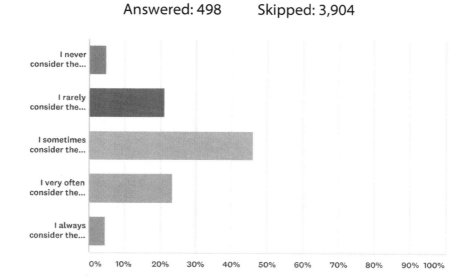

ANSWER CHOICES	RESPONSES	
I never consider the values/behaviors of the company producing products I purchase.	4.82%	24
I rarely consider the values/behaviors of the company producing products I purchase.	21.08%	105
I sometimes consider the values/behaviors of the company producing products I purchase.	45.98%	229
I very often consider the values/behaviors of the company producing products I purchase.	23.49%	117
I always consider the values/behaviors of the company producing products I purchase.	4.62%	23
TOTAL		498

Q14
Please indicate your level of agreement with the following statement: I am more willing to invest in or purchase products from companies if I believe there is a greater social purpose.

Answered: 496   Skipped: 3,906

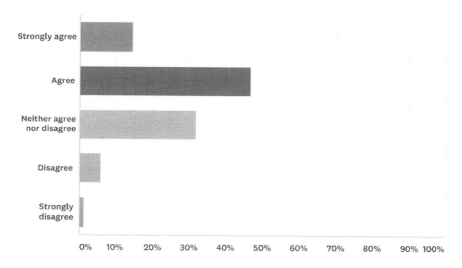

ANSWER CHOICES	RESPONSES	
Strongly agree	14.52%	72
Agree	46.57%	231
Neither agree nor disagree	31.85%	158
Disagree	5.85%	29
Strongly disagree	1.21%	6
TOTAL		496

Citations

[1] Koppel was perhaps best known for his work anchoring ABC's *Nightline* (1980-2005), which originated as a series of special reports on the Iranian hostage crisis.

[2] Gunnar Friede, Timo Busch, and Alexander Bassen, "ESG and Financial Performance: Aggregated Evidence From More than 2,000 Empirical Studies," *Journal of Sustainable Finance and Investment*, published December 19, 2015 (https://papers.ssrn.com/sol3/papers.cfm?abstract_id=2699610&mod=article_inline).

[3] Gunnar Friede, Timo Busch, and Alexander Bassen, "ESG and Financial Performance: Aggregated Evidence From More than 2,000 Empirical Studies," *Journal of Sustainable Finance and Investment*, published December 19, 2015 (https://papers.ssrn.com/sol3/papers.cfm?abstract_id=2699610&mod=article_inline).

[4] Jana Matthews, "Why Respecting Women as Purchasers is Key to Business Growth," *Entrepreneur.com*, published March 8, 2019 (https://www.entrepreneur.com/article/329780).

[5] Lou Carlozo "Female Financial Advisors Find Their Way," *U.S. News & World Report*, published July 12, 2017 (https://money.usnews.com/investing/articles/2017-07-12/female-financial-advisors-find-their-way)

[6] "14 Women Win the 2019 Top CEOs Award," glassdoor.com/blog, published June 18, 2019 (https://www.glassdoor.com/blog/top-women-ceos-2019/)

[7] Anne Stych, "Women's Representation on Boards Reaches a Milestone," Bizwomen, The Business Journals, published September 12, 2019 (https://www.bizjournals.com/bizwomen/news/latest-news/2019/09/womens-representation-on-boards-reaches-a.html?page=all)

[8] "Marketing to Women Quick Facts," sheconomy.com (http://she-conomy.com/report/marketing-to-women-quick-facts)

[9] Mary Beth Franklin, "One Place Where the Women Wealth Equation Doesn't Add Up," *Investment News*, published November 20, 2017 (https://www.investmentnews.com/article/20171120/FREE/171129995/one-place-where-the-women-wealth-equation-doesnt-add-up)

[10] "Financial Concerns of Women," BMO Wealth Institute, U.S. edition, published March 2015 (https://www.bmo.com/privatebank/pdf/Q1-2015-Wealth-Institute-Report-Financial-Concerns-of-Women.pdf)

[11] https://tradingeconomics.com/australia/gdp

[12] Donnie Borak, "U.S. deficit estimated to hit $1 trillion for 2020, CBO says," CNN.com, published August 21, 2019 (https://www.cnn.com/2019/08/21/politics/cbo-us-deficit-one-trillion/index.html)

[13] https://www.usdebtclock.org

[14] According to data from the U.S. Census Bureau cited in "7 Charts that Show the Glaring Gap Between Men and Women's Salaries in the U.S.," an article by Sonam Sheth, Shayanne Gal, and Andy Kiersz, *Business Insider,* published August 26, 2019 *(https://www.businessinsider.com/gender-wage-pay-gap-charts-2017-3)*

[15] "Women now control more than half of US personal wealth, which 'will only increase in years to come'," Gorman, Ryan, *Business Insider*, https://www.businessinsider.com/women-now-control-more-than-half-of-us-personal-wealth-2015-4

[16] Paula Span, "The Gray Gender Gap: Older Women Are Likelier to Go It Alone," The New York Times, published October 7, 2016 (https://www.nytimes.com/2016/10/11/health/marital-status-elderly-health.html)

[17] Heather Ettinger and Eileen M. O'Connor, "Women of Wealth Study," *Family and Wealth Advisors Council*, 2012 (https://familywealthadvisorscouncil.com/wp-content/uploads/FWAC-WomenOfWealth-2012.pdf)

[18] LouAnn Lofton, *Warren Buffett Invests Like a Girl: And Why You Should, Too*, HarperBusiness, published April 2012 (https://www.amazon.com/Warren-Buffett-Invests-Like-Girl/dp/0061727636)

[19] "Current U.S. Inflation Rates: 2009-2019" (https://www.usinflationcalculator.com/inflation/current-inflation-rates/)

[20] According to data from the U.S. Census Bureau cited in "7 Charts that Show the Glaring Gap Between Men and Women's Salaries in the US," an article by Sonam Sheth, Shayanne Gal, and Andy Kiersz, *Business Insider,* published August 26, 2019 *(https://www.businessinsider.com/gender-wage-pay-gap-charts-2017-3)*

[21] Yekaterina Chzhen, Anna Gromada, and Gwyther Rees, "Are the World's Richest Countries Family Friendly? Policy in the OECD and EU," published June 2019 (https://www.unicef-irc.org/publications/pdf/Family-Friendly-Policies-Research_UNICEF_%202019.pdf)

[22] "Despite Rising Influence, Women Report Steady Decline in Financial Confidence," published June 24, 2019 (https://www.allianzlife.com/about/newsroom/2019-press-releases/women-report-steady-decline-in-financial-confidence)

23 https://thequantum.com/financial-facts-for-womens-history-month/

24 https://thequantum.com/financial-facts-for-womens-history-month/

25 https://thequantum.com/financial-facts-for-womens-history-month/

26 https://www.catalyst.org/research/women-in-the-workforce-united-states/

27 https://www.catalyst.org/research/women-in-the-workforce-united-states/

28 https://www.fundera.com/resources/women-owned-business-statistics

29 "United States Net Worth Brackets, Percentiles, and Top One Percent," dqydj.com (https://dqydj.com/net-worth-brackets-wealth-brackets-one-percent/)

30 "Marketing to Women Quick Facts," sheconomy.com (http://she-con-omy.com/report/marketing-to-women-quick-facts)

31 Heather R. Ettinger and Eileen M. O'Connor, "Women of Wealth: Why Does the Financial Services Industry Still Not Hear Them?," *Family and Wealth Advisors Council*, 2012 (https://familywealthadvisorscouncil.com/wp-content/uploads/FWAC-WomenOfWealth-2012.pdf)

32 https://www.mckinsey.com/business-functions/organization/our-insights/delivering-through-diversity

33 Jie Chen, Woon Sau Leung, Wei Song, and Marc Goergen, "Research: When Women Are on Boards, Male CEOs Are Less Overconfident," *Harvard Business Review*, published September 12, 2019 (https://hbr.org/2019/09/research-when-women-are-on-boards-male-ceos-are-less-overconfident)

34 Beth Ann Bovino and Jason Gold, "The Key to Unlocking U.S. GDP Growth: Women," *S&P Global* (https://www.spglobal.com/en/research-insights/featured/the-key-to-unlocking-u-s-gdp-growth-women)

35 "The Ultimate List Of Charitable Giving Statistics For 2018, " *NP Source,* https://nonprofitssource.com/online-giving-statistics/

36 "The Ultimate List Of Charitable Giving Statistics For 2018, " *NP Source,* https://nonprofitssource.com/online-giving-statistics/

37 "Investment by Women, and in Them, is Growing," *The Economist,* published March 8, 2018 https://www.economist.com/finance-and-economics/2018/03/08/investment-by-women-and-in-them-is-growing

38 Morgan Stanley Institute for Sustainable Investing, "Sustainable Signals: New Data from the Individual Investor," 2017 (https://www.morganstanley.com/pub/content/dam/msdotcom/ideas/sustainable-signals/pdf/Sustainable_Signals_Whitepaper.pdf)

39 Susan Chira, "Money is Power. And Women Need More of Both," *New York Times*, published March 10, 2018 (https://www.nytimes.com/2018/03/10/sunday-review/women-money-politics-power.html)

[40] https://www.asyousow.org/about-us/theory-of-change

[41] Kimberly Chin, "Small Investors Punch Above Their Weight: Niche Investors Are Often Able to Spur Companies to Address ESG Issues," *The Wall Street Journal*, September 22, 2019, (https://www.wsj.com/articles/small-esg-investors-punch-above-their-weight-11569204180)

[42] https://news.gallup.com/poll/228281/satisfaction-government-remains-low.aspx

[43] Grace Haley, "Suburban Women Could Decide 2020: Who Are They Giving To?" OpenSecrets.org, published November 6, 2019 (https://www.opensecrets.org/news/reports/suburban-women-donors)

[44] Luisa Rollenhagen, "Everything You Need to Know About ESG Investing," *Wealthsimple* (https://www.wealthsimple.com/en-us/learn/esg-investing#why_choose_esg_investments)

[45] "John Wesley on Giving," (https://www.resourceumc.org/en/content/john-wesley-on-giving)

[46] "Dow Stock is Sold by Union Seminary," New York Times, 11 January 1969: 31.

[47] https://www.parametricportfolio.com/solutions/better-beta/responsible-investing

[48] https://www.asyousow.org/shareholder-advocacy-1

[49] According to the Governance and Accountability Institute, 85% of companies in the S&P 500 publish such reports (https://www.ga-institute.com/press-releases/article/flash-report-85-of-sp-500-indexR-companies-publish-sustainability-reports-in-2017.html)

[50] Billy Nauman, "Credit Rating Agencies Join Battle for ESG Supremacy," *The Financial Times,* published September 16, 2019 (https://www.ft.com/content/59f60306-d671-11e9-8367-807ebd53ab77)

[51] Ivana Kottosova, "Volkswagen's Diesel Scandal Costs Hit $33 Billion with New Audi Penalty," *CNN Business*, published October 16, 2018 (https://www.cnn.com/2018/10/16/business/volkswagen-audi-diesel-fine/index.html)

[52] "United Airlines Changes Policy After 'horrific' Passenger Ordeal," *BBC.com*, published April 16, 2017 (https://www.bbc.com/news/world-us-canada-39617879)

[53] Jie Chen, et al, "Why female board representation matters: The role of female directors in reducing male CEO overconfidence," *Science Direct,* Vol. 53, September 2019, pp. 70-90 (https://www.sciencedirect.com/science/article/abs/pii/S0927539819300520#!)

[54] https://marketbusinessnews.com/financial-glossary/esg-definition-meaning/

[55] Ryan Vlastelica, "U.S. Stock Trading Hit a Three-Year Low in 2017 Amid Near-Absent Volatility," MarketWatch, published December 22, 2017 (https://www.marketwatch.com/story/us-stock-trading-volume-hit-a-three-year-low-in-2017-amid-near-absent-volatility-2017-12-21)

[56] Jon Quigley and Lyn Taylor, "The Impact of Negative Screening," Financial Advisor Magazine, published February 1, 2010 (https://www.fa-mag.com/news/the-impact-of-negative-screening-5062.html)

[57] Gunnar Friede, Timo Busch, and Alexander Bassen, "ESG and Financial Performance: Aggregated Evidence from More than 2,000 Empirical Studies," *Journal of Sustainable Finance and Investment*, published December 19, 2015 (https://papers.ssrn.com/sol3/papers.cfm?abstract_id=2699610&mod=article_inline)

[58] "Report on Sustainable, Responsible, and Impact Investing Trends 2018," *The Forum for Sustainable and Responsible Investing* (https://www.ussif.org/files/Trends/Trends%202018%20executive%20summary%20FINAL.pdf)

[59] Isobel Owen, "Do women really make better investors than men?" The Financial Times, published April 30, 2019 (https://www.ft.com/content/f3835072-66a6-11e9-9adc-98bf1d35a056)

[60] Isobel Owen, "Do women really make better investors than men?" The Financial Times, published April 30, 2019 (https://www.ft.com/content/f3835072-66a6-11e9-9adc-98bf1d35a056)

[61] LouAnn Lofton, Warren Buffett Invests Like a Girl: And Why You Should, Too, HarperBusiness (April 2012) (https://www.amazon.com/Warren-Buffett-Invests-Like-Girl/dp/0061727636)

[62] Lou Carlozo "Female Financial Advisors Find Their Way," U.S. News & World Report, published July 12, 2017 (https://money.usnews.com/investing/articles/2017-07-12/female-financial-advisors-find-their-way)

[63] "POLL: How Americans Would Spend an Extra $1,000," Lexington Law, published August 3, 2018 (https://www.lexingtonlaw.com/blog/news/how-americans-would-spend-1000-survey.html)

[64] Claer Barrett, "Best of Money: Why Do Women Fear the Stock Market?" The Financial Times, published June 3, 2016 (https://www.ft.com/content/b681b8e6-2705-11e6-8b18-91555f2f4fde)

[65] Amy Brown, "On ESG and Impact Investing, More Women are Leading the Charge," Triple Pundit, published April 11, 2019 (https://www.triplepundit.com/story/2019/esg-and-impact-investing-more-women-are-leading-charge/83131/)

[66] https://www.ussif.org/staff

67 Ellie Zhu and James Gallardo, "Female Advisors More Likely to Consider ESG Investing Strategies," Investment News, published November 19, 2018 (https://www.investmentnews.com/article/20181119/BLOG18/181119912/female-advisers-more-likely-to-consider-esg-investing-strategies)

68 Maggie Fox, "FDA Launches New Anti-Vaping Campaign Aimed at Teens," NBCnews.com (https://www.nbcnews.com/health/health-news/fda-launches-anti-vaping-campaign-aimed-teens-n910691)

69 Justin Green, "The Global Anti-Vaping Tipping Point," Axios.com (https://www.axios.com/vaping-regulations-movement-juul-1f160084-cdc9-44fd-a1d6-560717518b62.html)

70 "Report on Sustainable, Responsible, and Impact Investing Trends 2018," The Forum for Sustainable and Responsible Investing (https://www.ussif.org/files/Trends/Trends%202018%20executive%20summary%20FINAL.pdf)

71 "Monster Beverage Corporation—A Case Study in Shifting from Laggard to Leader on Slavery in Supply Chain," As You Sow Press Release, published June 4, 2019 (https://www.asyousow.org/press-releases/monster-beverage-slavery-supply-chain)

72 "General Mills Outlines Strategies for Reducing Pesticide Use in Supply Chain," As You Sow Press Release, published August 15, 2019 (https://www.asyousow.org/press-releases/2019/8/15/general-mills-pesticide-use)

73 https://www.asyousow.org/invest-your-values/

74 https://www.asyousow.org/about-us

75 https://www.asyousow.org/resolutions-tracker

76 https://www.parnassus.com/esg#introduction

77 "MSCI ESG Ratings May Help Identify Warning Signs," Shareholder Advocacy: As You Sow (https://www.msci.com/documents/1296102/6174917/MSCI-ESG-Ratings-Equifax.pdf/b95045f2-5470-bd51-8844-717dab9808b9)

78 Georg Kell, "The Remarkable Rise of ESG," Forbes.com, published July 11, 2018 (https://www.forbes.com/sites/georgkell/2018/07/11/the-remarkable-rise-of-esg/#1ecd86bb1695)

79 Lou Carlozo, "Female Financial Advisors Find Their Way," U.S. News and World Report, published July 12, 2017 (https://money.usnews.com/investing/articles/2017-07-12/female-financial-advisors-find-their-way)

80 Sylvia Ann Hewlett and Andrea Turner Moffitt, "The Financial Services Industry's Untapped Market," Harvard Business Review, published December 8, 2014 (https://hbr.org/2014/12/the-financial-services-industrys-untapped-market)

[81] Michael Cannivet, "Why Women Are Better At Investing," *Forbes.com*, published December 29, 2018 (https://www.forbes.com/sites/michaelcannivet/2018/12/29/why-women-are-better-at-investing/#56658aa36f37)

[82] "Investment By Women, and In Them, is Growing," *The Economist*, published March 8, 2018 (https://www.economist.com/finance-and-economics/2018/03/08/investment-by-women-and-in-them-is-growing)

[83] Ellie Zhu and James Gallardo, "Female Advisors More Likely to Consider ESG Investing Strategies," InvestmentNews, published November 19, 2018 (https://www.investmentnews.com/article/20181119/BLOG18/181119912/female-advisers-more-likely-to-consider-esg-investing-strategies)

[84] "Asset Manager Climate Scorecard 2018," 50/50 Climate Project (https://5050climate.org/wp-content/uploads/2018/09/FINAL-2018-Climate-Scorecard-1.pdf)

[85] "Report on US Sustainable, Responsible and Impact Investing Trends 2018," The Forum for Sustainable and Responsible Investing (https://www.us-sif.org/files/Trends/Trends%202018%20executive%20summary%20FINAL.pdf)

[86] "Report on US Sustainable, Responsible, and Impact Investing Trends 2018," The Forum for Sustainable and Responsible Investing (https://www.us-sif.org/files/Trends/Trends%202018%20executive%20summary%20FINAL.pdf)

[87] Mark Miller, "Bit By Bit, Socially Conscious Investors Are Influencing 401(k)'s," The New York Times, published September 27, 2019 (https://www.nytimes.com/2019/09/27/business/esg-401k-investing-retirement.html)

[88] "Gender Parity on Boards Around the World," *Harvard Law School Forum on Corporate Governance and Financial Regulation*, published January 5, 2017 (https://corpgov.law.harvard.edu/2017/01/05/gender-parity-on-boards-around-the-world/)

[89] Rachel Feintzeig, "Women's Share of Board Seats Rises to 20%," *The Wall Street Journal*, published September 11, 2019 (https://www.wsj.com/articles/womens-share-of-board-seats-rises-to-20-11568194200)

[90] "Moving the Needle on Gender Parity Through Active Ownership," https://www.parametricportfolio.com/investor-challenges/moving-the-needle-on-gender-parity-through-active-ownership

[91] Gavin Power, "ESG Investing and Fixed Income: The Next New Normal?" *Pimco.com*, published June 2018 https://global.pimco.com/en-gbl/insights/viewpoints/esg-investing-and-fixed-income-the-next-new-normal)

[92] Ron Surz, "U.S. Stock Market Is Biggest and Most Expensive In World, But U.S. Economy is Not the Most Productive," nasdaq.com, published April 2,

2018 (https://www.nasdaq.com/articles/us-stock-market-biggest-most-expensive-world-us-economy-not-most-productive-2018-04-02)

[93] Steven Melendez, "Bond Market Size vs. Stock Market Size," Zacks Finance, updated March 6, 2019 (https://finance.zacks.com/bond-market-size-vs-stock-market-size-5863.html)

[94] Gavin Power, "ESG Investing and Fixed Income: The Next New Normal?" Pimco.com, published June 2018 (https://global.pimco.com/en-gbl/insights/viewpoints/esg-investing-and-fixed-income-the-next-new-normal)

[95] Emily E. Robare, Spotlight on ESG Opportunities: This City Is Powered by 100% Renewable Energy https://www.gurtin.com/blog/spotlight-on-esg-opportunities-renewable-energy/

[96] Per Sierra Club - https://www.sierraclub.org/ready-for-100

[97] Dale Ross, "Commentary: I'm Georgetown mayor. We raise a glass to renewable energy," The Austin-American Statesman, published August 11, 2018 (https://www.statesman.com/news/20180811/commentary-im-georgetown-mayor-we-raise-a-glass-to-renewable-energy)

[98] Matt Wirz, "Climate-Activist Countries Fuel Record Year for Green Bonds," *The Wall Street Journal*, published October 25, 2019 (https://www.wsj.com/articles/climate-activist-countries-fuel-record-year-for-green-bonds-11572004800)

[99] https://charts.ussif.org/sam/?StrategyType=BON&

[100] Thea Okin, "Municipals and Responsible Investing: A Natural Fit," Western Asset (https://www.westernasset.com/us/en/research/blog/esg-2019-07-26.cfm)

[101] Betty Moy Huber, Michael Comstock and Hilary Smith, Davis Polk & Wardwell LLP, "UN Sustainable Development Goals--The Leading ESG Framework for Large Corporations," October 4, 2018 (https://corpgov.law.harvard.edu/2018/10/04/un-sustainable-development-goals-the-leading-esg-framework-for-large-companies/)

[102] Eleanor Laise, "Can Sustainable Bonds Change the World?" *Kiplinger*, published July 29, 2019 (https://www.kiplinger.com/article/retirement/T052-C000-S004-can-sustainable-bonds-save-the-world.html)

[103] Jay Ashar, "Goldman Sachs Launches Sustainable Finance Group," *The Global Treasurer*, (https://www.theglobaltreasurer.com/2019/07/26/goldman-sachs-launches-sustainable-finance-group/)

[104] Adam Tempkin, "Freddie Mac Targeting ESG Investors with Green Mortgage Bonds," *Bloomberg Online*, published June 10, 2019 (https://www.bloomberg.com/news/articles/2019-06-10/freddie-mac-targeting-esg-investors-with-green-mortgage-bonds)

[105] Kevin McPartland, "Understanding the $41 Trillion U.S. Bond Market," *Forbes.com*, published October 11, 2018 (https://www.forbes.com/sites/kevinmcpartland/2018/10/11/understanding-us-bond-market/#7ae0e1f81caf)

[106] Maria Municchi, "How Should ESG Investors Think About Government Bonds?" *Episodeblog*, published May 19, 2019 (https://www.episodeblog.com/2019/05/20/how-should-esg-investors-think-about-government-bonds/)

[107] Thea Okin, "Municipals and Responsible Investing—A Natural Fit," *Western Asset* (https://www.westernasset.com/us/en/research/blog/esg-2019-07-26.cfm)

[108] "Corporate Bonds vs. Municipal Bonds," *The Motley Fool*, published January 13, 2017 (https://www.fool.com/knowledge-center/corporate-bonds-vs-municipal-bonds.aspx)

[109] http://www.msrb.org/msrb1/pdfs/MSRB-Muni-Facts.pdf

[110] "From Evolution to Revolution: 10 Years of Green Bonds," Worldbank.org, published November 27, 2018 (https://www.worldbank.org/en/news/feature/2018/11/27/from-evolution-to-revolution-10-years-of-green-bonds)

[111] "From Evolution to Revolution: 10 Years of Green Bonds," Worldbank.org, published November 27, 2018 (https://www.worldbank.org/en/news/feature/2018/11/27/from-evolution-to-revolution-10-years-of-green-bonds)

[112] Mark Miller, "Bit By Bit, Socially Conscious Investors Are Influencing 401(k)'s," The New York Times, published September 27, 2019 (https://www.nytimes.com/2019/09/27/business/esg-401k-investing-retirement.html)

[113] According to data from the U.S. Census Bureau cited in "7 Charts that Show the Glaring Gap Between Men and Women's Salaries in the U.S.," an article by Sonam Sheth, Shayanne Gal, and Andy Kiersz, *Business Insider,* August 26, 2019 *(https://www.businessinsider.com/gender-wage-pay-gap-charts-2017-3)*

[114] For a complete summary of the survey results, see https://drive.google.com/file/d/1VAiDn0n3vsmF3zzNAy8GvEmjDebjhCR1/view?usp=sharing

Made in the USA
Middletown, DE
15 August 2020